REFLECTIONS

VAN EYCK AND THE PRE-RAPHAELITES

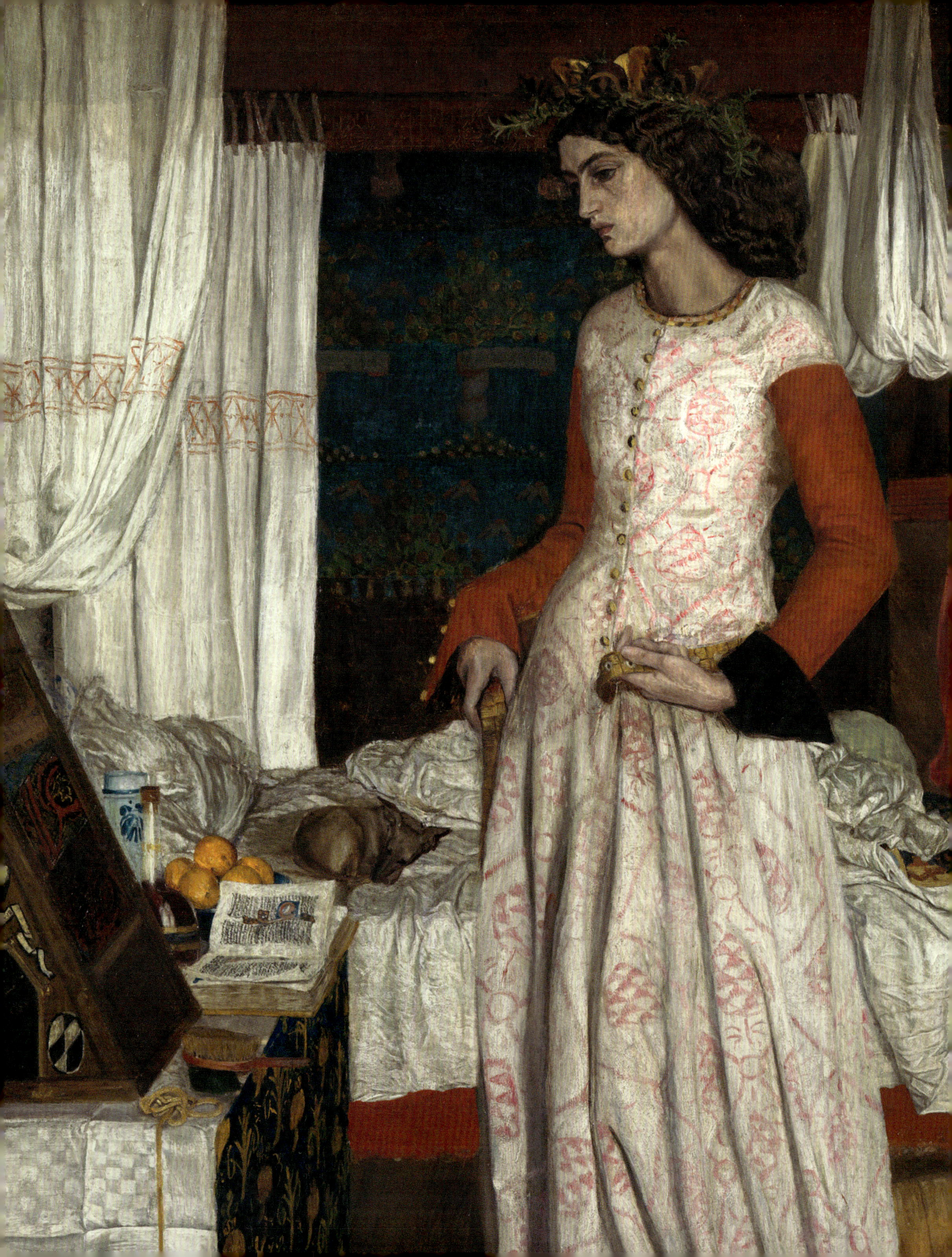

REFLECTIONS

VAN EYCK AND THE PRE-RAPHAELITES

Alison Smith
with Caroline Bugler, Susan Foister
and Anna Koopstra

National Gallery Company, London
Distributed by Yale University Press

Published to accompany the exhibition

REFLECTIONS

VAN EYCK AND THE PRE-RAPHAELITES

The National Gallery, London
2 October 2017 to 2 April 2018
Exhibition organised by the National Gallery in collaboration with Tate Britain

Exhibition generously supported by The Thompson Family Charitable Trust

COCKAYNE The London Community Foundation

And other members of the *Reflections: Van Eyck and the Pre-Raphaelites* Exhibition Supporters Circle.

The Sunley Room exhibition programme is supported by The Bernard Sunley Charitable Foundation.

This exhibition has been made possible by the provision of insurance through the Government Indemnity Scheme. The National Gallery would like to thank HM Government for providing Government Indemnity and the Department for Culture, Media and Sport and Arts Council England for arranging the indemnity.

Front cover:

John Everett Millais (1829–1896)
Mariana, 1851
Tate, London. Accepted by HM Government in lieu of tax and allocated to the Tate Gallery 1999 (T07553)
Detail of Cat. 16

Back cover:

Jan van Eyck (active 1422; died 1441)
Portrait of Giovanni (?) Arnolfini and his Wife ('The Arnolfini Portrait'), 1434
Detail of Cat. 1

Page 2:

William Morris (1834–1896)
La Belle Iseult, 1857–8
Tate, London. Bequeathed by Miss May Morris 1939 (N04999)
Detail of Cat. 20

CONTENTS

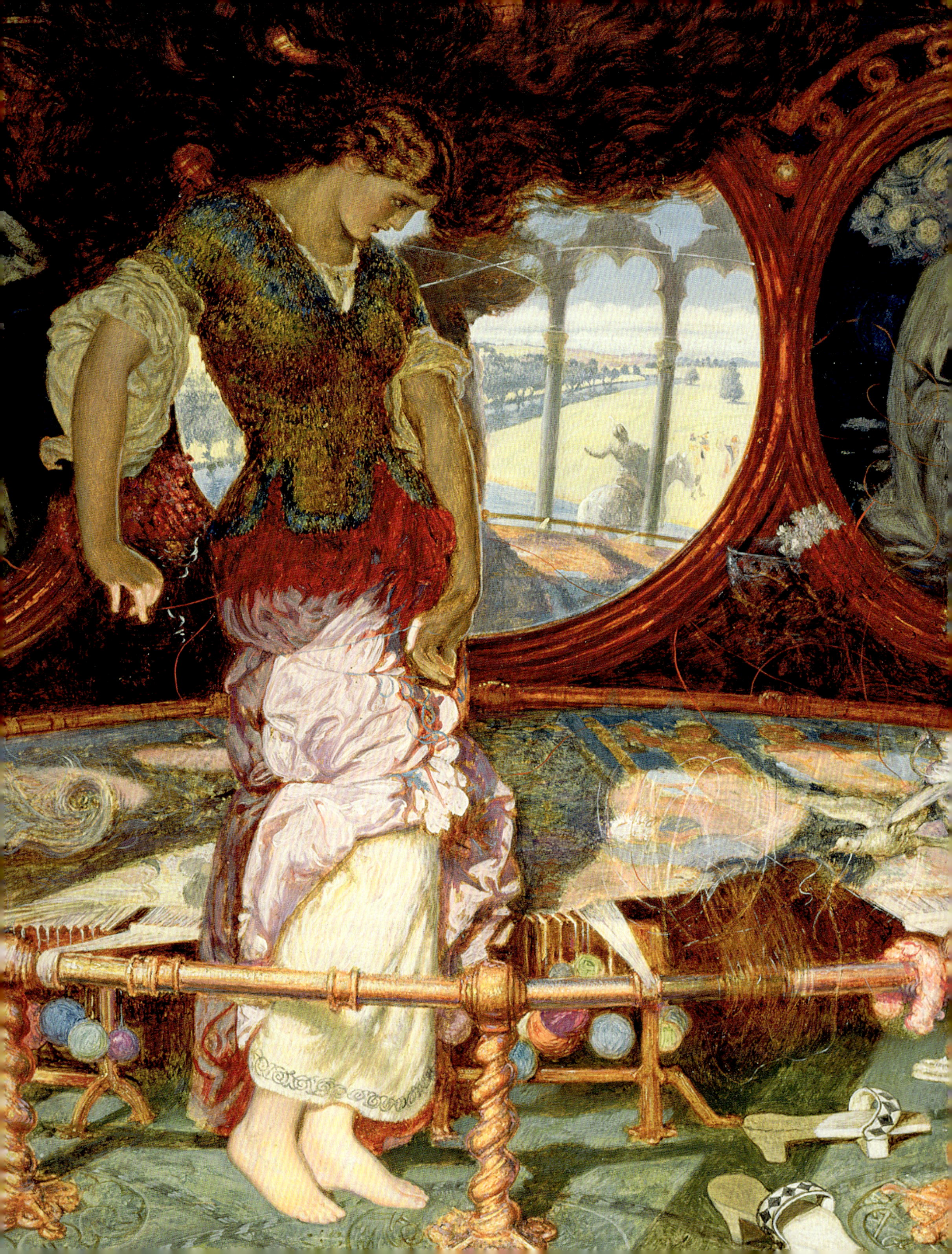

PREFACE

Fig. 1, detail of Cat. 31, p. 59

When Jan van Eyck's *Arnolfini Portrait* was acquired for the National Gallery in 1842 it was the first early painting from the Low Countries to enter the collection. At the time it was not a famous picture, but it attracted instant admiration. Two woodcut illustrations of it appeared in the British press in 1843, and one critic compared its precise rendition of natural appearances to the effects achieved by the recently invented daguerreotype.

More significantly though, it made a deep impression on three young artists who were studying at the Royal Academy Schools which then occupied the east side of the Gallery building, just a few yards from where the picture hung: William Holman Hunt, Dante Gabriel Rossetti and John Everett Millais. As founder members of the Pre-Raphaelite Brotherhood in 1848, they created richly coloured, highly wrought pictures of deeply serious subjects, characterised by an overriding concern for fidelity to nature and an obsessive attention to detail. Burne-Jones, a later adherent of Pre-Raphaelite ideas, declared that as a young man he had stood in front of the *Arnolfini Portrait* and determined to paint pictures with similar intense colours and beautiful finish.

Reflections: Van Eyck and the Pre-Raphaelites explores this relationship as well as the mesmerising influence that the convex mirror in the *Arnolfini Portrait* exercised on two generations of British painters fascinated both by its technical virtuosity and its symbolic potential. Conceived by Alison Smith and Susan Foister, curators at Tate Britain and the National Gallery respectively, the exhibition is the reflection of a very close collaboration between our two institutions. It received a strong initial impetus from Penelope Curtis when she was Director of Tate Britain, and has benefited from ongoing support at Tate with particular thanks to Caroline Collier and Gillian Buttimer. We are grateful to all the lenders who have made their works available for the exhibition.

At the National Gallery we would like to acknowledge the generous support of The Thompson Family Charitable Trust, The Bernard Sunley Charitable Foundation, Cockayne – Grants for the Arts, The London Community Foundation and other members of the *Reflections: Van Eyck and the Pre-Raphaelites* Exhibition Supporters' Circle.

Gabriele Finaldi, *Director, The National Gallery*
Alex Farquharson, *Director, Tate Britain*

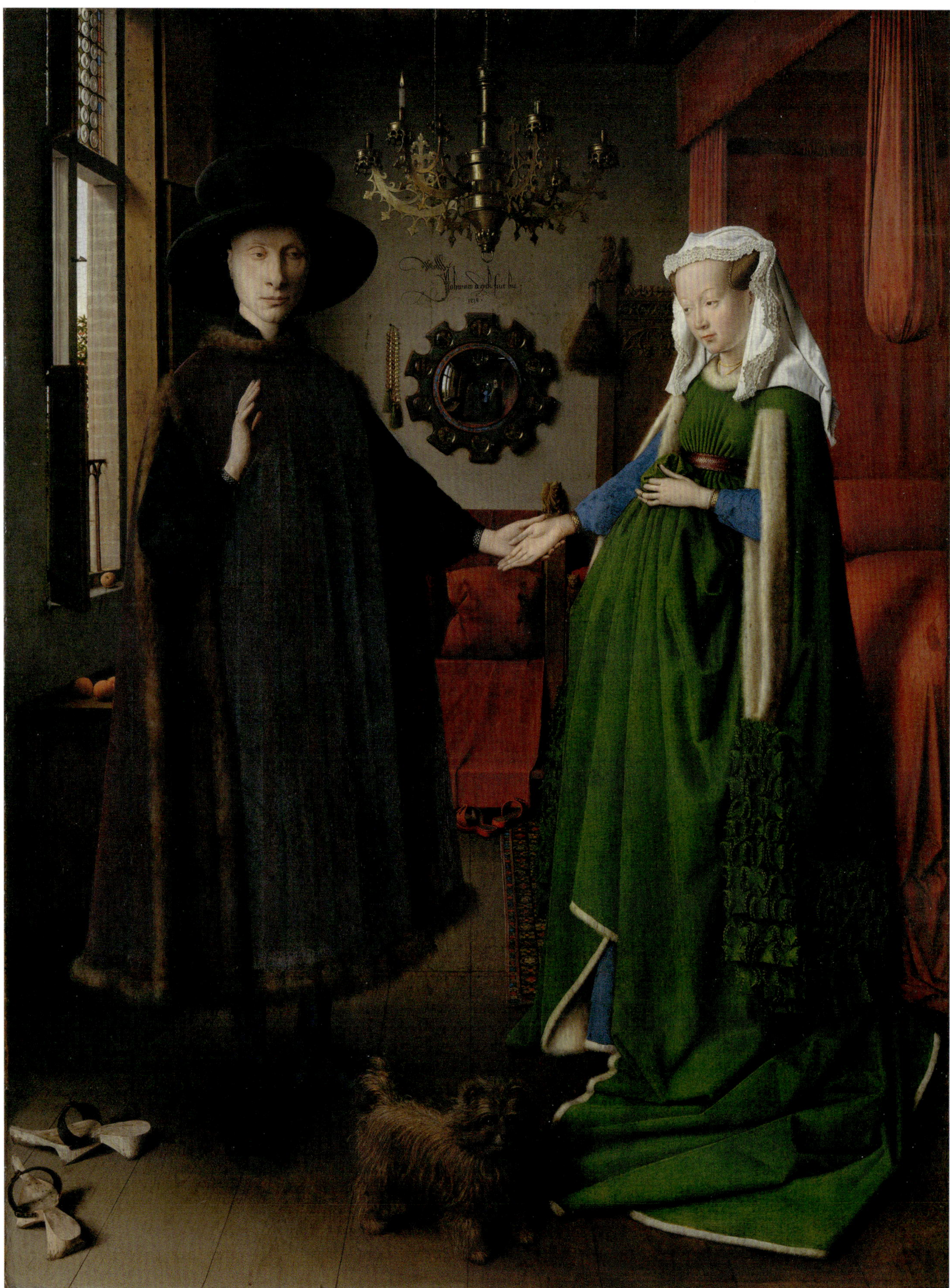

JAN VAN EYCK'S ARNOLFINI PORTRAIT

Susan Foister

Cat. 1
Jan van Eyck (active 1422; died 1441)
Portrait of Giovanni(?) Arnolfini and his Wife ('The Arnolfini Portrait'), 1434
Oil on oak, 82.2 × 60 cm
The National Gallery, London. Bought, 1842 (NG 186)

Jan van Eyck, who died in Bruges in 1441, was famous in Europe in his own time, and has been acknowledged as one of the greatest painters ever since. That his reputation has remained so high in more recent times is not least because of the presence of the *Arnolfini Portrait* (cat. 1) in the National Gallery, one of the most popular paintings in the collection, and one that has attained a cult-like status through the successive re-imaginings of artists.

Unlike many of his contemporaries in the Low Countries, van Eyck consistently signed and dated his works, a feature that must have helped to recommend his *Arnolfini Portrait* to the National Gallery Trustees, who acquired it in 1842. The Gallery's sole example of painting from this place and period, and in excellent condition, it was perceived as a perfect document of the art of oil painting, which van Eyck was then erroneously believed to have invented. Today it is recognised that the medium of oil paint had been employed for some centuries before van Eyck's lifetime.[1] Yet the sophistication of the manner in which he used it, and the astonishing representational effects he achieved, were unparalleled: in the *Arnolfini Portrait* for example he used not only his paintbrush but his fingers to soften the shadow of the dog, and to blot the green glaze of the woman's dress, and frequently worked at speed, applying fresh layers of wet paint before the previous layers had dried. Despite the clarity of detail in this small painting his effects are often suggestive and his technique economical rather than laboured.

The National Gallery's collection includes two further van Eycks: in 1851 it added *Portrait of a Man (Self Portrait?),* dated 1433 (cat. 2), and in 1857 *Portrait of a Man (Léal Souvenir),* dated 1432.[2] These are all small works, as are many of

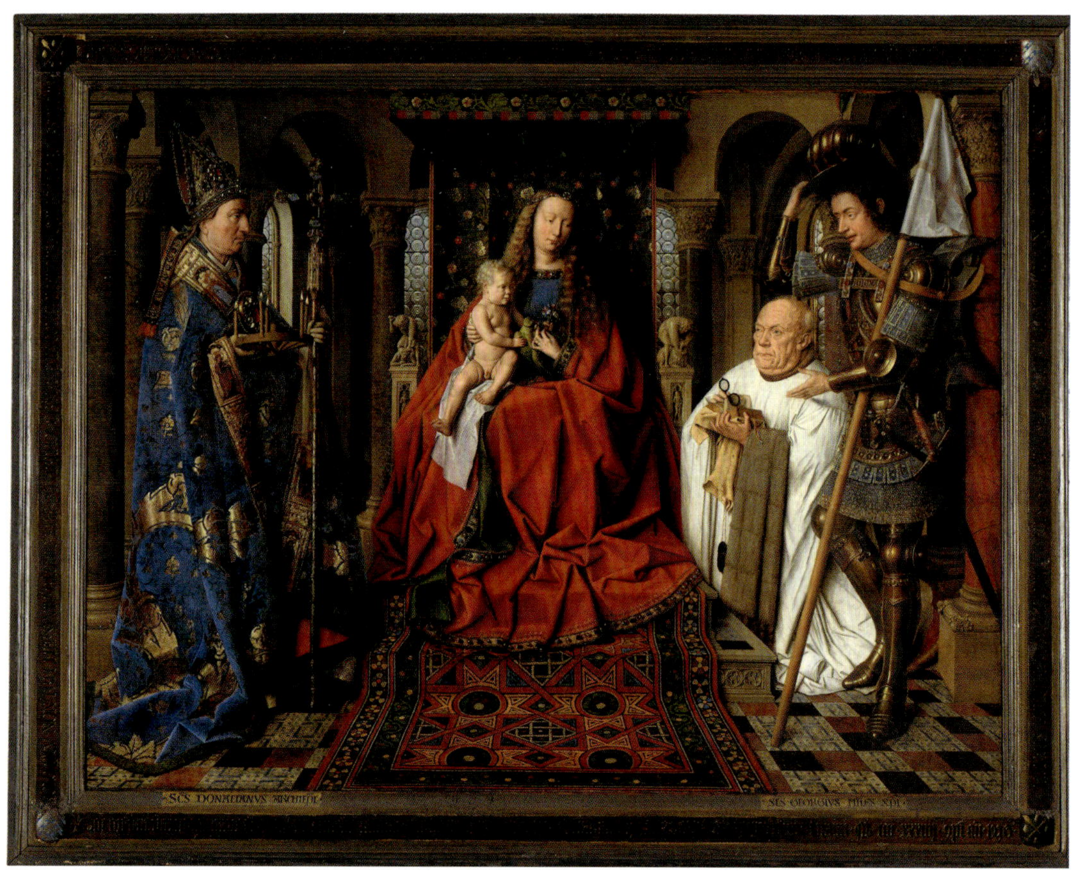

Fig. 2
Jan van Eyck (active 1422; died 1441)
Virgin and Child with Saints Donation and George and Canon van der Paele, about 1434–6
Oil on wood, 122 × 156 cm
Groeningemuseum, Stedelijke Musea Brugge, Bruges

van Eyck's devotional paintings and portraits in other collections, but he also painted on a larger scale, as seen in *The Virgin and Child with Saints Donation and George and Canon van der Paele* in Bruges (fig. 2), and completed the vast *Ghent Altarpiece* begun by his brother Hubert (fig. 3). Like many of his contemporaries, van Eyck made work for a range of patrons, but his outstanding abilities were recognised above all by Philip the Good, Duke of Burgundy, who made him his *varlet de chambre* (equerry) and paid him an exceptional salary.

The *Arnolfini Portrait,* which is dated 1434, shows a couple standing with linked hands in an interior. The man and woman have been identified as members of the Arnolfini family, merchants from Lucca in Italy, who traded in Bruges. As early as 1516, in the first known reference to the painting, they were identified as 'Hernoul le Fin' with his wife. The man is probably Giovanni di Nicolao Arnolfini, who was still living in Bruges in 1452. He had married the well-connected Costanza Trenta in 1426; she died before 26 February 1433 (possibly long before this date), and though there is no record of a second marriage, it is likely that Giovanni married again, and that the portrait shows his second wife.

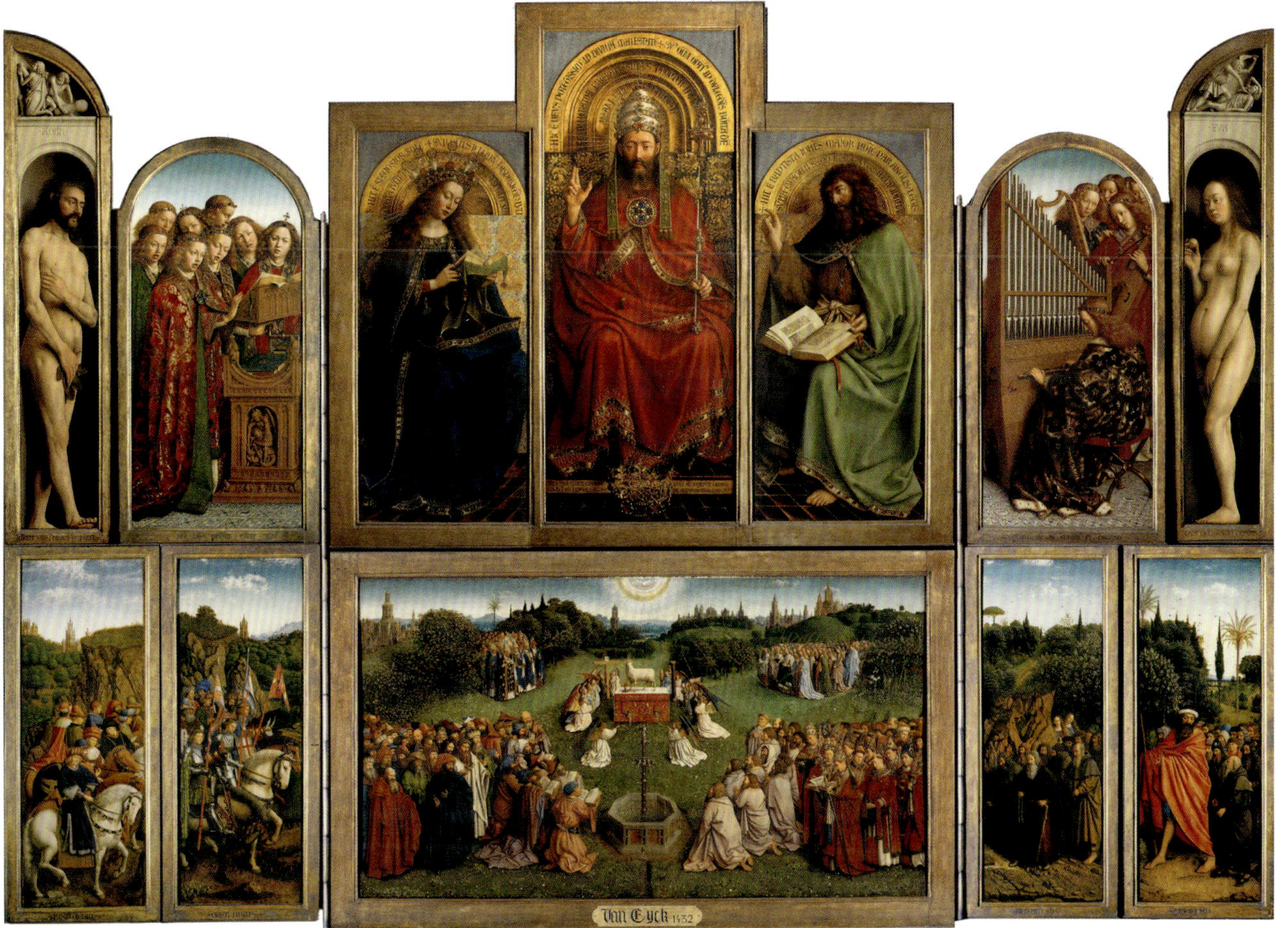

Fig. 3
Hubert van Eyck (died 1426) and **Jan van Eyck** (active 1422; died 1441)
The Ghent Altarpiece (inner face, open)
Oil on wood, 350 cm × 460 cm
St Bavo, Ghent

Arnolfini wears a weighty fur-lined velvet tabard, originally purple in colour. His black hat is made of straw. On his feet are pointed boots and, next to them, dirt-stained wooden pattens for outdoor wear. His wife wears a very long green gown, looped up over her stomach. It is lined with white fur, and the visible hanging sleeve is slashed and stitched in a complex pattern. Her hair is fashionably plaited and dressed as two horns covered in red netting, with a layered white linen veil arranged over it. Accompanying the two figures is a small dog with a shaggy grey-brown pelt. The figures stand in a room illuminated by an open window, the upper part of which is glazed with small panes. Outside the branches of a cherry tree in fruit are visible. On the window sill and chest below are oranges, then expensive, exotic fruit. Behind the figures to the right is a bed, an item that featured in many living rooms of the period. On the adjacent chair is a carved figure of Saint Margaret and her identifying attribute, the dragon, and above this hangs a clothes brush. Overhead is an elaborate brass chandelier holding a single lit candle. But perhaps the most notable feature of the painting, which has attracted most attention and commentary, is the circular mirror, next to which hangs a string of prayer beads.

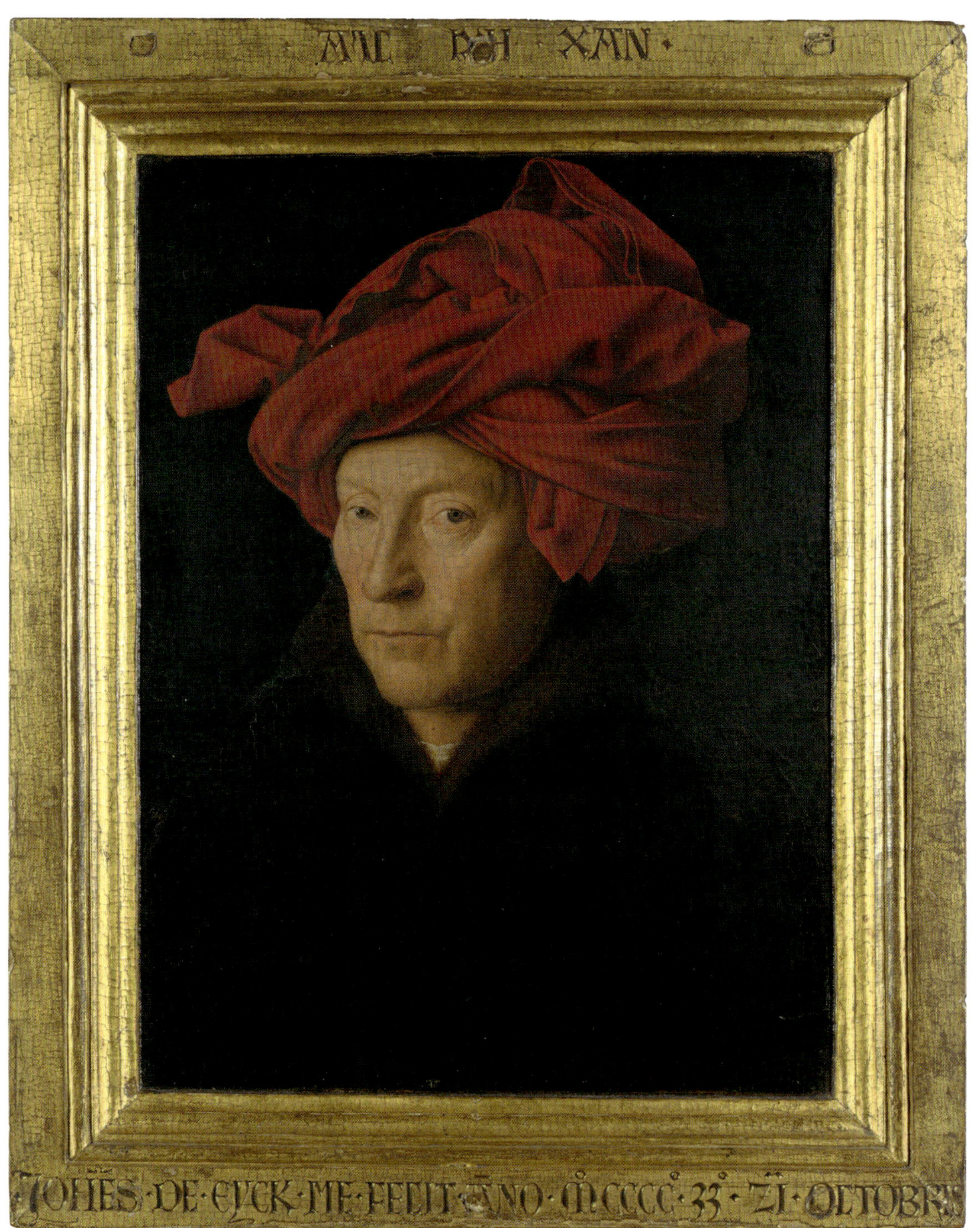
IOHES · DE · EYCK · ME · FECIT · ANO · MCCCC · 33 · 21 · OCTOBRIS

Cat. 2
Jan van Eyck (active 1422; died 1441)
Portrait of a Man (Self Portrait?), 1433
Oil on oak, 26 × 19 cm
The National Gallery, London.
Bought, 1851 (NG 222)

The mirror frame has ten small circular painted scenes of the Passion of Christ arranged around it. Reflected in its convex surface are the backs of the two figures represented in the painting and, between them, as though entering the room in the viewer's place, are two male figures, the foremost, in blue, raising his arm as he steps forward. Above the mirror is an inscription in Latin as though graffitied on the wall, which translates as 'Jan van Eyck has been here. 1434'. The implication is not only that the man in blue is the artist but that van Eyck is the extraordinarily skilful author of what is depicted.

Various theories have been advanced over the centuries about the subject of the painting. In 1568 the chronicler Marcus van Vaernewijck wrote that the picture showed the 'marriage of a man and a woman who are married by faith'. In 1599 Jakob Quelviz described the picture as showing a couple joining hands as if promising future marriage. In the following century it was described as showing a pregnant German woman getting married by night. In 1855 de Laborde again took up the marriage theory, and the notion of the pregnant bride; he identified the figures in the mirror as the witnesses.[3] In the twentieth century the art historian Erwin Panofsky greatly elaborated this theory, postulating that the candle was a marriage candle, that the man was raising his right hand to take a matrimonial oath, that his shoes were removed because he was on holy ground, and that the painting constituted a kind of marriage certificate.[4] In the National Gallery's most recent catalogue entry on the painting, published in 1998, Lorne Campbell argues that it is a sophisticated portrait made for a couple with whom the artist was on friendly terms, tolerating the intrusive signature. Using the evidence of underdrawing, which shows van Eyck changing the gestures, he suggests that the raised hand is a greeting to the artist. The bulky dress worn by the female sitter is typical of the period, and was also worn by female saints, who could not have been pregnant.[5]

Assessing the work of Jan van Eyck and this portrait in particular is not straightforward, owing to the rarity of surviving paintings by contemporaries and predecessors. Examples of portraits and of paintings of secular subjects are greatly outweighed by religious images, yet study of manuscript illuminations and tapestries of the period indicates that secular imagery and full-length portraiture were not at all unusual, and van Eyck must have drawn on such visual traditions to create his compelling interior. Any suggestion that his portrait reflects the ways in which devotional texts may have informed paintings with religious subjects and invested objects depicted in them with symbolic meaning is, however, far more speculative. The carved figure of Saint Margaret for instance represents the patron saint of pregnancy and childbirth, but if the female sitter is not pregnant then the significance of the figure is greatly diminished, and it may simply be an indication of the opulence of the Italian merchant's environment. Van Eyck represents the objects in the room with such vividness that it is not surprising that viewers – and perhaps artists in particular – have wished to endow them with a symbolic significance and resonance. Not the least of these objects is the mirror, and van Eyck's attraction to reflective surfaces such as the polished brass of the chandelier and the glass beads suspended by the mirror, as well as the convex glass of the mirror itself and the glazing protecting the small paintings surrounding it, must have derived from his intense interest in the ways oil paint could be manipulated to suggest such optical qualities. Although not every instance of the inclusion of a reflective mirror in a fifteenth-century work of art necessarily pays homage to the *Arnolfini Portrait,* there is no doubt that the work was frequently referenced in its time, and that few painters have matched van Eyck's remarkable skill in evoking reflections.

In 1516 the painting was in the collection of Margaret of Austria at Mechelen.[6] An inventory records that it was given to her by Don Diego de Guevara, a Spanish nobleman brought up at the Burgundian court. The inventory also mentions that the painting then had two shutters, with the coat of arms and device of Don Diego; this does not exclude the possibility that the painting originally had shutters, which were then repainted with the details of the subsequent owner. It passed to Margaret's niece, Mary of Hungary, who left the Low Countries for Spain in 1556, where she died two years later in 1558. Her effects passed to her nephew, King Philip II of Spain (1527–1598). In the Spanish royal collections it would have been seen by Diego Velázquez, who became court painter to King Philip IV in 1628, and died in Madrid in 1660 (see p. 67). The painting is next recorded in the inventory of King Charles II of Spain after his death in 1700, still in the Alcázar palace at Madrid. In 1794 it was in the Palacio Nuevo in Madrid. At some point in the Peninsular War it appears that a Scottish soldier, James Hay, acquired the painting, possibly when the baggage train of Joseph Bonaparte fell into the hands of the Duke of Wellington at the Battle of Vitoria in 1813, although Hay later told how he saw and admired it when convalescing at a house in Brussels. It was Hay who subsequently offered it unsuccessfully to the Prince Regent in 1816 and, much later in 1842, successfully to the Trustees of the National Gallery.

THE ARNOLFINI PORTRAIT IN THE NINETEENTH CENTURY
RECEPTION AND REPRODUCTION

Anna Koopstra

When James Hay brought the *Arnolfini Portrait* to Britain after the defeat of Napoleon, he opened a new chapter in its history. Given the unprecedented dispersal of works of art that resulted from Napoleon's wars,[1] it seems somehow fitting that after Hay sold it the picture went on display in a new museum on Trafalgar Square, a public space named after one of the battles against the French fleet. The painting's arrival in Britain, which marked a decisive break with its past, also coincided with a period of rapid change in Europe; in the early nineteenth century, societies were being transformed by political and social events and advances in technology.

The public exhibition of works of art and the rise of the popular press – which both met and stimulated a growing interest in art – played a significant role in the National Gallery's acquisition of the *Arnolfini Portrait* in 1842. At that point, the picture had already been in the country for over 20 years. In a memorandum from 1865 (cat. 3) Colonel Hay's friend James Wardrop recalled that Hay sent him the picture to keep while he was away: 'It was hung up between two windows in a bed room where it remained, I believe about thirteen years, during which period it was seen by many visitors, none of whom deemed [the picture] worthy of any particular notice.'[2] It was not until its first public appearance in the 1841 Old Master exhibition at the British Institution in London that the work was remarked upon, in particular by the art critic George Darley (1795–1846). In his informed review for the *Athenaeum* of 3 July 1841 he discussed the 'Portraits of a Gentleman and a Lady' by 'John' van Eyck, 'a great name' (and moreover a 'true one',

NGA02/4/2/228

Memorandum

The Van Eyck was sent to me by Col. James Hay, in charge to keep for him during his absence.

It was hung up between two windows in a Bed room where it remained, I believe about thirteen years, during which period it was seen by many visitors, none of whom deemed it worthy of any particular notice.

After the lapse of this time

4852
8499

NG5/50/1

Treasury Chambers
May 2nd 1842

My Lords & Gentlemen

In reply to the letters addressed by your Secretary to this Board by your direction on the 8th March and 28th ultimo, I am commanded by the Lords Commissioners of Her Majesty's Treasury to acquaint you, that, under the present circumstances of the Country, My Lords cannot recommend to Parliament to grant so large a sum as £10,300 for the purchase of Pictures for the National Gallery. But as My Lords have reason to believe that there are some particular circumstances connected with the picture by Van Eyck, which render it desirable that that picture should be acquired

for

Cat. 3

Memorandum written by James Wardrop, 1865

The National Gallery Archive, London (NGA02/4/2/228)

Cat. 4

Treasury letter, dated May 2 1842, stating that the Lords would recommend to Parliament the purchase of the *Arnolfini Portrait*.

The National Gallery Archive, London (NG5/50/1)

Cat. 5

The Illustrated London News, April 1843

Bound volume (Jan–June 1843)

Museum of London (74.335/1)

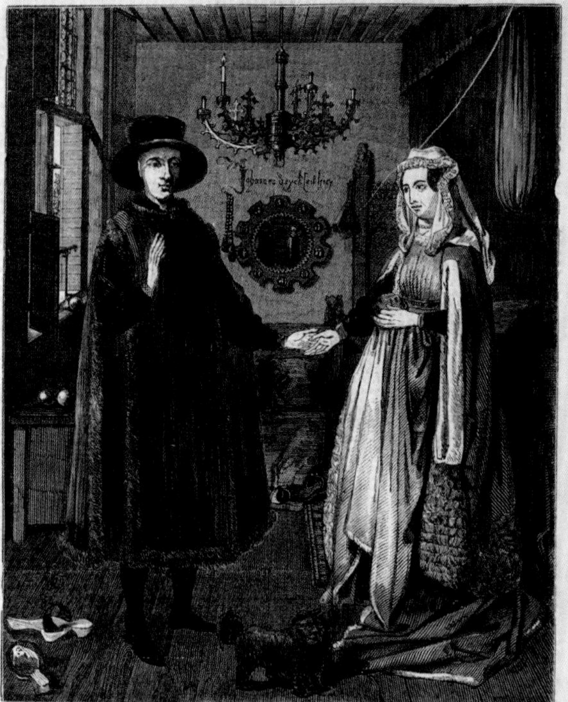

"Johannes de Eyck fecit hic,
1434." *Inscription on the picture.*

VAN EYCK'S PICTURE IN THE NATIONAL GALLERY.

open air, and all its deleterious influences. The Van Eyck seems to have been protected, and to owe its freshness to some process of this kind.

The "discovery"—or rather we should say the improved re-discovery—of oil painting, of which this remarkable picture stands as one of the principal monuments, consisted, says Vasari, in his "Lives of Most Excellent Painters," and published in Florence, 1550, in "nothing more than this:—according to the ancient practice, a fresh colour was never added to the panel until the first covering had been dried in the sun; a mode infinitely tedious, and one in which the colours could never perfectly harmonize. Van Eyck saw this difficulty, and he became more truly sensible of it from the circumstance of having exposed one of his paintings to the sun in order to harden, when the excess of heat split the panel. Being at that period sufficiently skilled in philosophical inquiries, he began to speculate on the manner of applying oils, and of their acquiring a proper consistency without the aid of the sun. By uniting it with other mixtures he next produced a varnish, which, dried, was waterproof, and gave a clearness and brilliancy while it added to the harmony of his colours." The oils used by him are said to have been "linseed and nut oils, boiled." "Before the time of Van Eyck," says Lanzi, "some sort of painting in oil was known, but so extremely tedious and imperfect as to be scarcely applicable to the production of figure pieces. It was practised beyond the Alps," and, we may add, by the Egyptians of the Greek period, of which a most remarkable specimen may be seen in the Louvre; "but it is not known to have been in use in Italy." Giovanni carried the first discovery to its completion; he perfected the art, which was afterwards diffused over all Europe, and introduced into Italy by Antonello da Messina.

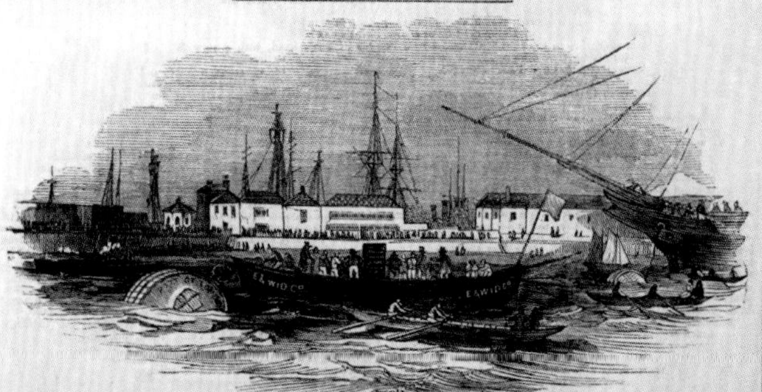

DIVING AT BLACKWALL.

The attempt to recover the body of Mr. Busfield was renewed on Saturday morning last, at ebb tide, by a large number of watermen, who successively dragged all those points of the river where the current sets in strongest from Blackwall to Bugsby's-hole. The offer made on Friday by Mr. Knight, the chief superintendent of the East India Dock Company, to allow the use of their diving apparatus for the purpose of examining the mooring-chains which cross the river in several places near Blackwall, was gladly accepted by the relatives of the deceased, and the barge containing the necessary machinery was brought round from the West India Dock basin, and moored off the pier before seven o'clock on Saturday morning. The helmet diving apparatus, invented by Deane, and successfully employed at Spithead and other places, was considered more suitable for the purpose than the diving-bell; and Thomas Jones, an experienced diver, in the service of the Eas and West India Dock Company, was selected to perform the arduous task. The weather was very unfavourable for the attempt, the wind blowing strong from the south-west, and causing a heavy swell in the reach. Before nine o'clock, however, everything was in readiness for the first descent. Jones having adjusted the helmet and enveloped himself in a waterproof dress, descended the ladder to make an examination of the piles near the western end, among which it was considered very probable that the deceased might have been entangled. After remaining under water more than half an hour, Jones returned to the surface, and reported that he had carefully examined along the whole range of piles, and could discover nothing of the body.

The novelty of the machinery, and the melancholy occasion of its employment, contributed to attract an immense number of persons to the spot; but one feeling of regret at the unfortunate occurrence appeared to animate every breast, and the most perfect order prevailed. The barge having been made fast to the buoy, Jones prepared to descend once more. The usual weight of his dress was considerably increased, in order to counteract the effect of the current, which sets in strongly against the pier at all times of the tide. The leaden weights suspended to various parts of his person amounted to nearly a hundred and a half weight; but even this was barely sufficient to carry him safely through the current. Jones remained under water for a great length of time, and eventually walked from the northern buoy to the Essex shore, along the line of chain: his researches, however, were unfortunately of no avail.

It will be recollected that when a young female, a domestic servant in the Duke of Buccleuch's family, lost her life by falling from the same pier in landing out of a Scotch steamer, her body remained under water for six weeks, and was eventually brought to the surface by one of the ballast-lighters.

Since Sunday every exertion has been made to discover the body. On Tuesday morning, as soon as it was low water, Jones recommenced his labour, and continued with but little intermission until the tide turned, examining the various holes and bed of the river. At high water he was compelled to abandon his exertions; but as soon as the tide turned he re-descended, when he proceeded to the buoys on the Essex shore, without meeting the object of his search. At each time he rose a piece of ordnance which was placed on a barge moored opposite the pier was fired eight or ten times, it being anticipated that the vibration would cause the body to float, provided it was not entangled. The diving and firing continued up to near 5 o'clock, when further attempts were abandoned. During the whole of these melancholy proceedings an innumerable number of boats were rowing about in all directions, for the purpose of picking up the body if it should float. The failure of these experiments leads to the supposition that the remains of the deceased gentleman are carried beyond the lower reaches.

POPULAR PORTRAITS.—No. XXXVII.

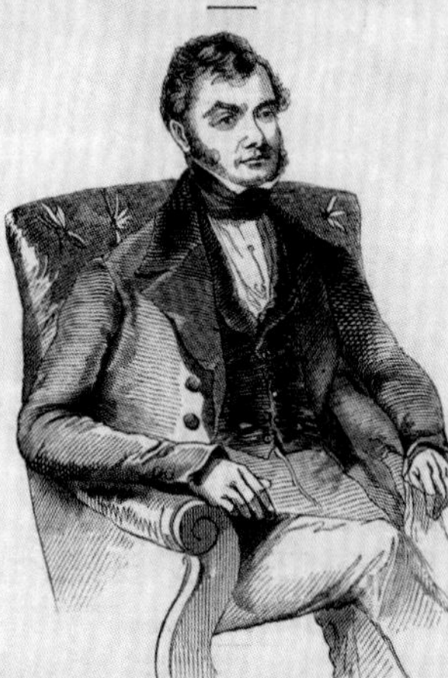

HOWARD ELPHINSTONE, Esq., M.P.

There is another accession to the ranks of the Anti-Corn-law League in the person of Howard Elphinstone, Esq., the member for the borough of Lewes. From his entrance into Parliament he has been known as a free-trader; but it is not every one holding, in his station, those opinions, who joins openly in the operations of the League itself. They agree in the object to be attained, but differ as to the means of attaining it. Mr. Elphinstone concurs both in means and object, and has embarked thoroughly in the cause. At the Drury Lane meeting on Wednesday evening last he was one of the principal speakers. It has been said that the study of the law generally induces a preference for the forms and usages of the past, and a repugnance to change which throws many of our greatest lawyers into the ranks of the Conservative party. Mr. Elphinstone appears to be an exception; he is a doctor of civil law, and practices as an advocate at Doctors' Commons. He is therefore immersed in the intricacies of our ecclesiastical courts and their forms of procedure, which partake more of the spirit of the past than any part of our legal system, and yet he is a supporter, in his political capacity, of many things which the admirer of old things—the *laudator temporis acti*—would shrink from in fear and terror; in the house Mr., or rather Dr., Elphinstone votes for the ballot, short Parliaments, extension of the suffrage, and (as evinced by his last speech) the repeal of the Corn-laws, and free trade in its fullest signification. Dr. Lushington, who is a judge in the same courts, is also well known as a Liberal in politics.

Dr. Elphinstone is the descendant of a house that has given the country warriors both by sea and land: his grandfather was the Admiral Elphinstone who defeated the Turkish fleet at the battle of Tchesmé; he is the son of Major-General Sir Howard Elphinstone. In addition to his professional rank as an advocate, he is a magistrate and deputy-lieutenant for the county of Sussex. He was first returned to Parliament for the borough of Hastings, in 1835, and represented it till 1837; in that year he contested Liverpool, but unsuccessfully; he first sat for Lewes in 1841.

CHRIST'S HOSPITAL.—We understand that those gentlemen who have engaged to act as stewards on the ensuing anniversary (23rd October) of the birthday of King Edward VI. have made application to the governors for permission to have its celebration held on this occasion in the large hall, in order to afford to those persons who have received the liberal advantages of this excellent institute the opportunity of testifying their gratitude, and cordially acknowledging the munificent favours which royalty has recently so bounteously bestowed upon that foundation. The governors having, on a previous occasion, kindly granted the use of the hall for the benefit of another charity, but which had no immediate connection with their own, we may confidently anticipate that this request, preferred as it is upon such laudable motives, will be most willingly acceded to.

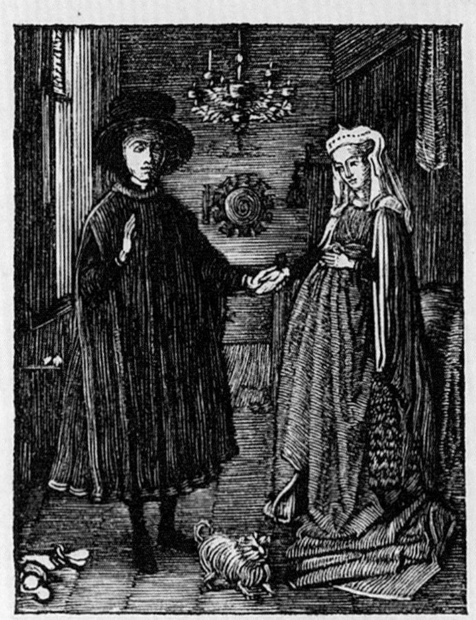

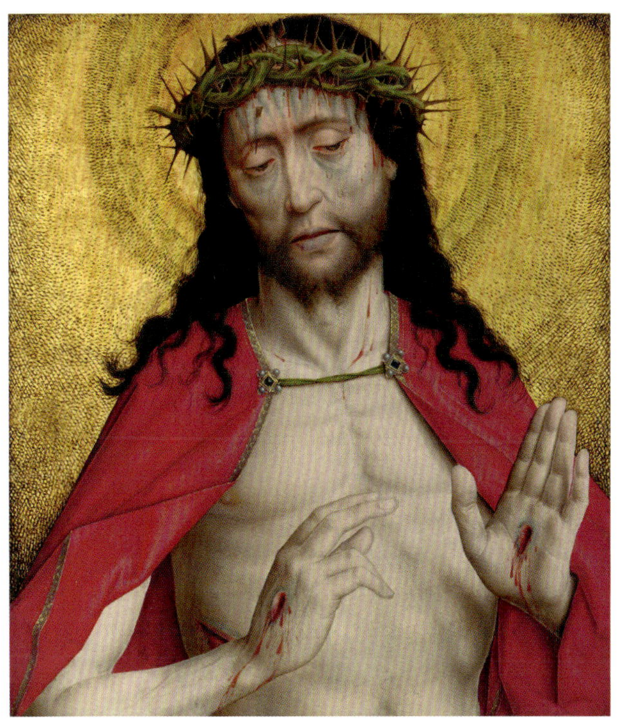

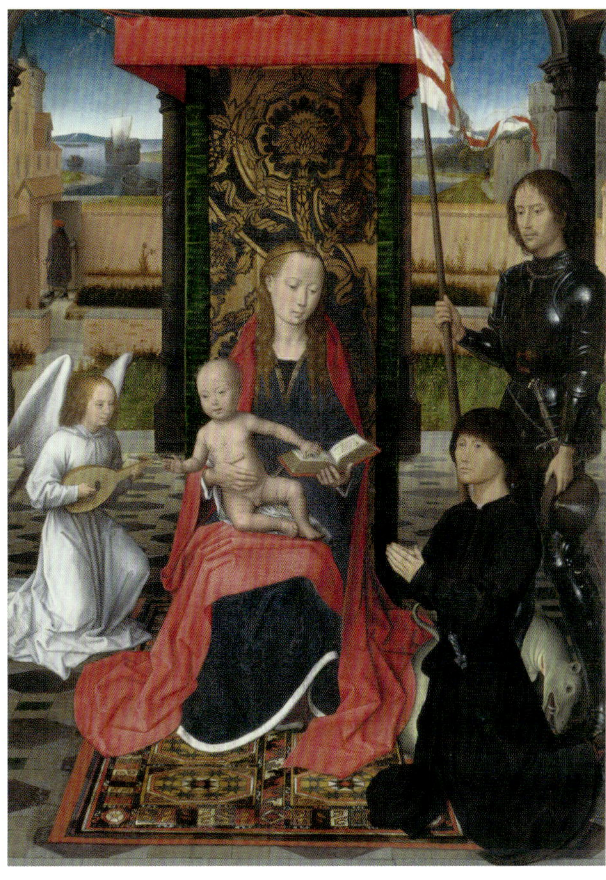

Cat. 6

Woodcut of the *Arnolfini Portrait* by the Linnell brothers, on page 49 of *Felix Summerly's Handbook for the National Gallery*. London: G. Bell, 1843.

The National Gallery Library, London (109455)

Cat. 7

Dirk Bouts (1400?–1475)

Christ Crowned with Thorns, about 1470

Oil with egg tempera on canvas backed onto board, transferred from wood, 43.8 × 37.1 cm

The National Gallery, London. Bequeathed by Mrs Joseph H. Green, 1880 (NG 1083)

Cat. 8

Hans Memling (active 1465; died 1494)

The Virgin and Child with an Angel, Saint George and a Donor, about 1480

Oil on oak, 54.2 × 37.4 cm

The National Gallery, London. Bought, 1862 (NG 686)

by which he meant that the painting, unlike many others, was undoubtedly by van Eyck because of its recognisable style and the fact that it carried a signature). The following year the portrait became the 186th work to be added to the collection of the National Gallery, which had been founded less than two decades earlier, in 1824.

A glimpse of the acquisition process can be caught from the minutes of the Trustees' meeting of 2 May 1842, which record that 'the Trustees are of opinion that the extraordinary merit of the Picture by Van Eyck, its perfect preservation, its extreme rarity and the moderate price at which it may be obtained, viz 600 guineas, moves them to recommend it without hesitation to my Lords as a valuable addition to the National Collection…'[3] In a response dated the same day (cat. 4; letters had been exchanged beforehand) the Treasury informed the Trustees that, although the 'circumstances of the Country' did not allow them to allocate the National Gallery the large sum of £10,300 for the purchase of pictures, they were willing to make an exception and pay for the van Eyck. The price appears to have been a decisive factor, 'as my Lords have reason to believe that there are some particular circumstances connected with the picture by Van Eyck, which render it desirable that that picture should be acquired for the public, their lordships would be willing to make provision for the purchase of it, on being informed of the manner in which

Cat. 9

Reproduction of the *Ghent Altarpiece* by Hubert van Eyck (died 1426) and Jan van Eyck (active 1422; died 1441), 1868–71

Chromolithograph plates in a black frame, 150 × 100 cm

The Maas Gallery

Cat. 10

Edward Burne-Jones (1833–1898)

Sketchbook, with drawings of decorative details, some from the *Ghent Altarpiece* by Hubert and Jan van Eyck, after 1859

Pencil and watercolour on paper (bound volume; in leather), 19.1 × 26.4 cm

Victoria and Albert Museum, London. Given by Dr W.L. Hildburgh F.S.A (E.4-1955)

it has been ascertained that the sum demanded for it is not beyond that which the merits of the picture entitle the party [Hay] to demand.'[4]

As soon as the *Arnolfini Portrait* went on display (by March 1843) it continued to attract attention. It was viewed not just by the critics and connoisseurs who formed the small circle of the London art world, but also by artists studying at the Royal Academy Schools (which until its move to Burlington House in 1869 shared a building with the National Gallery, see fig. 8, p. 32), as well as the general public, the 'men, women and children being admitted without distinction' for whom the gallery had been founded, and who were admitted free of charge. Its acquisition by the National Gallery thus marks another break in the history of the painting – a change of audience. For much of its 400-year history the portrait had belonged to private patrons and royal collections, where it was seen by a limited number of privileged viewers, but now it could be admired by more people than ever before.[5]

Technological developments in the reproduction of images further helped to introduce the portrait to a wider audience. In 1843 two woodcuts of the painting were published: one by an unknown maker was reproduced in the *Illustrated London News* (cat. 5), which had been founded the year before as the first weekly to carry illustrated news; the other, made by the artist John Linnell (1792–1882), appeared in *Felix Summerly's Handbook for the National Gallery* (cat. 6).[6] These prints – distributed via modern mass media though themselves executed in a centuries-old reproductive technique – were the first full copies ever made of the painting. In comparison, the *Ghent Altarpiece*, the largest and most important (see p. 10 and fig. 3), had been copied on a 1:1 scale by painters as early as the middle of the sixteenth century.

One such painted copy could be seen from 1819 onwards in London, where it was a prized work in the notable collection of the German merchant Carl Aders (1780–1846).[7] Aders's collection, which was frequented by the cultural elite of the time, played a key role in the developing taste for early Netherlandish painting in England. In addition to the *Ghent Altarpiece* copy, Aders possessed works by most of the great Northern 'Primitives': Rogier van der Weyden, Hans Memling, Gerard David and Dirk Bouts. No fewer than seven works by Bouts and his workshop were acquired by the National Gallery in the second half of the nineteenth century, including his *Christ Crowned with Thorns* (cat. 7), which had once belonged to Aders.

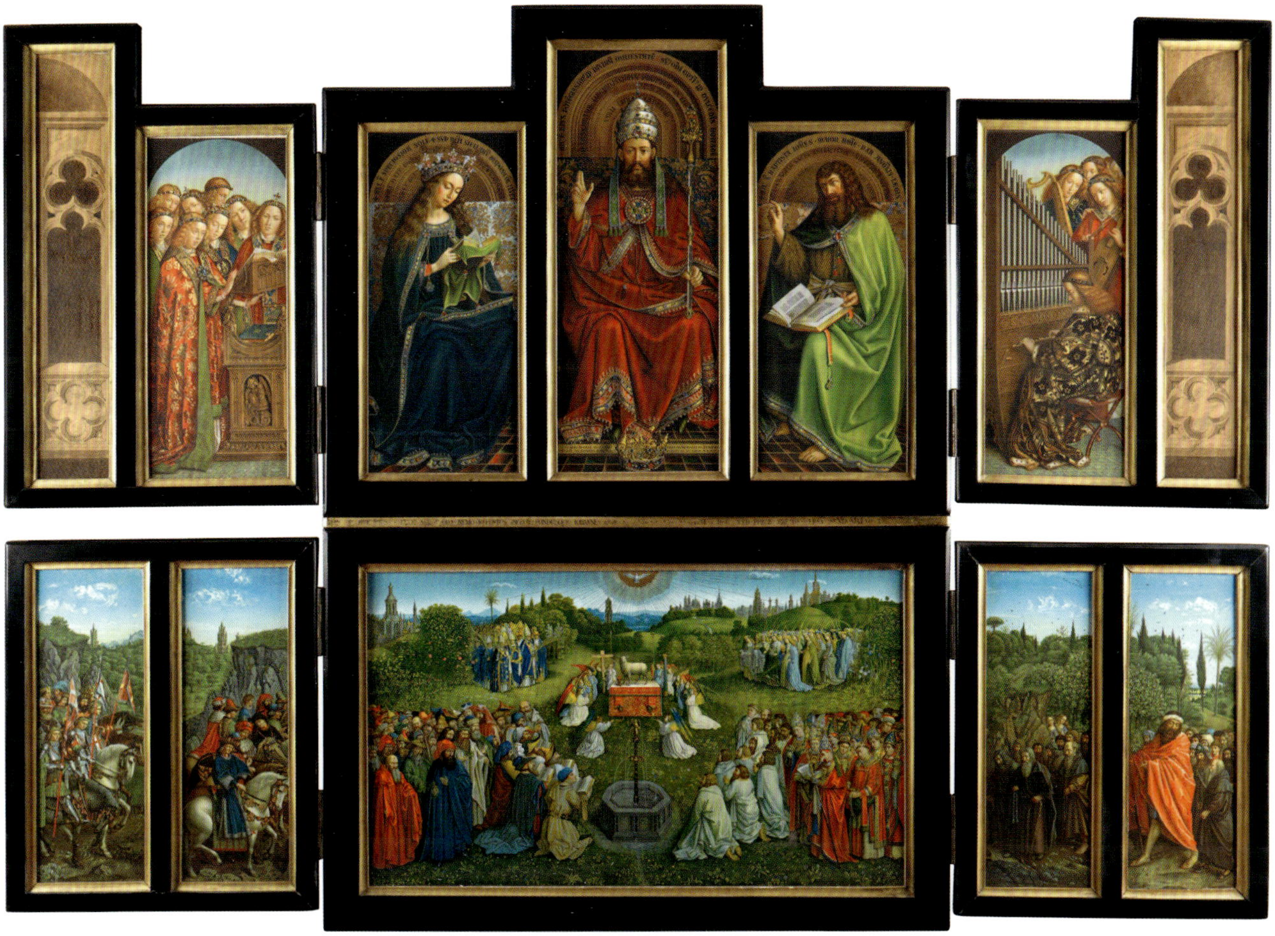

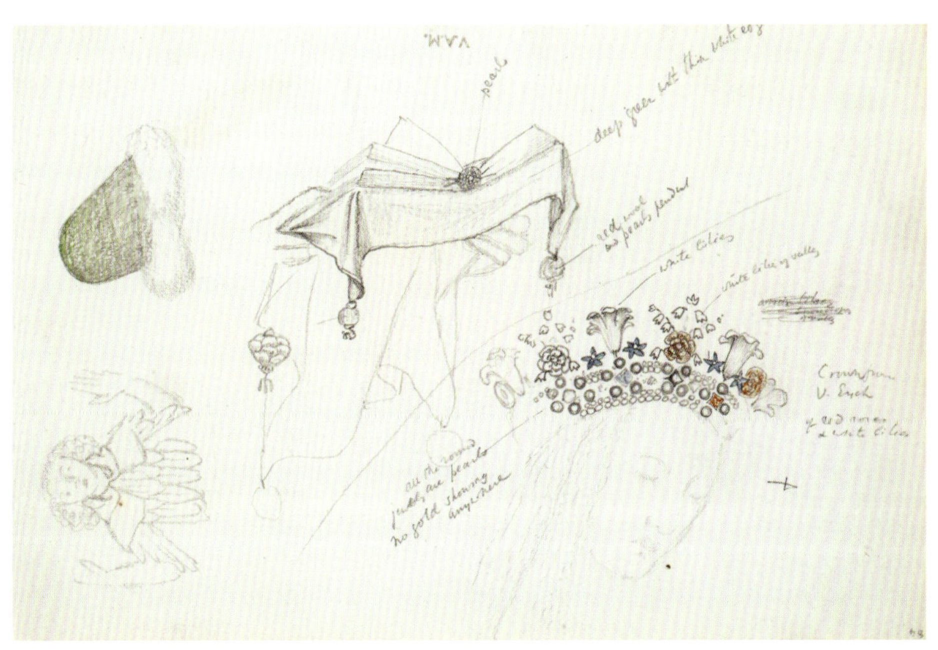
pearl
deep green with thin white edge
white lilies
white lilies of valley
Crown from V. Eyck
of red roses & white lilies
All the round jewels are pearls no gold showing anywhere

Hans Memling was also highly regarded. The first of his paintings to enter the National Gallery's collection was *The Virgin and Child with an Angel, Saint George and a Donor* (cat. 8), acquired in 1862. Memling's attraction lay in the perceived serenity of his style, which was held to reflect spirituality, a notion that resonated well with the Romantic values of the time. His popularity was possibly also influenced by the fact that a fair number of his pictures could be studied in Bruges, the city where he (and van Eyck) had lived and worked, which was visited by interested connoisseurs and artists alike, often along with other cities such as Antwerp and Ghent. For those who did not travel, the reproduction of works of art was of key importance. Edward Burne-Jones's sketches of several decorative details from the *Ghent Altarpiece*, for example, were probably made after reproductions (cat. 10).[8] The importance of disseminating knowledge of great works of art by copying and reproducing them can also be traced through the publications of the Arundel Society which, from its foundation in 1848, was dedicated to bringing Old Masters to the attention of an audience of art lovers. Between 1868 and 1871 it published the first colour reproductions of the Ghent altarpiece (cat. 9), made possible by chromolithography, a short-lived mass-printing technique.[9]

In 1839 the pioneers Louis Daguerre (1787–1851) and Henry Fox Talbot (1800–1877) had produced the very first photographs; by the second half of the century the middle classes could have their photos taken in studios specialising in portraits, as can be seen in early daguerreotypes depicting pairs (cats 11, 12). The *Arnolfini Portrait* thus fitted perfectly with current interests, both in style and subject matter; as early as 1843 van Eyck's picture was being compared to a photograph ('The various traceries, the border-and-scroll work, the enriched minor details of the room, seem to be *daguerrótyped rather than painted,* such is their extreme fineness and precision....').[10]

The appeal of the *Arnolfini Portrait* to the nineteenth-century viewer lay primarily in the 'realism' of its technique and its pristine condition, which was of special interest at the time since the quick degradation of the materials used in contemporary pictures was hotly debated. George Darley in his 1841 review elaborated on the authenticity and preservation of the picture before briefly concluding: 'Nevertheless, its merits are few besides those of colour and finish.' He further speculated about the morality of the relationship of 'this strange pair' by stating that they 'resemble nothing better than Simon Pure about to atone for a faux-pas by making Sarah Prim an honest woman', alluding to the fact that the latter appears pregnant (though he admits much of this is due to the 'old-fashioned costume').[11]

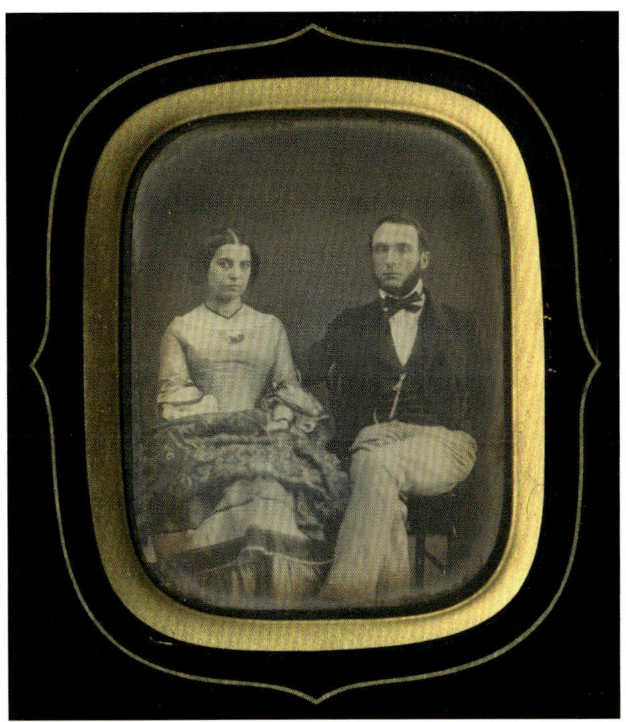

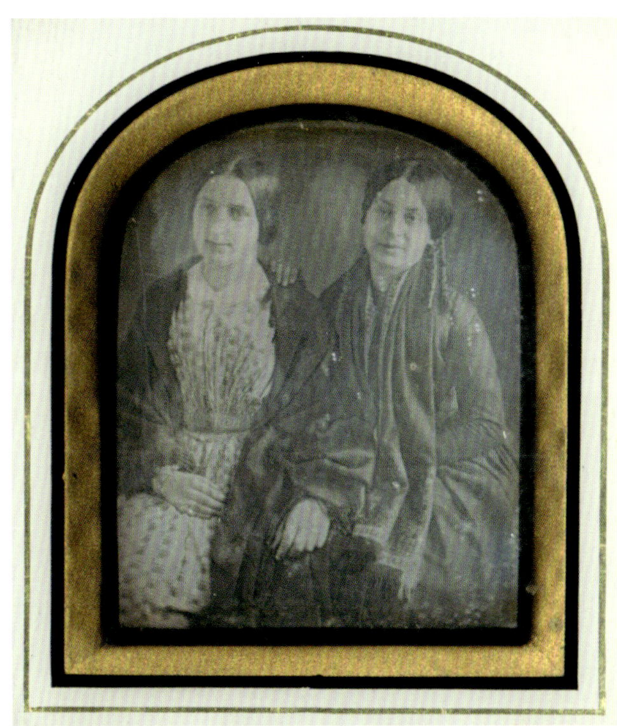

Cat. 11

Laubier, Paris

Léo François Louis de Mestral and his wife Léonie de Banes de Gardonne, about 1856

Gold-toned daguerreotype, 9.4 × 7 cm

Wilson Centre for Photography, London (12:1418)

Cat. 12

Anonymous photographer (thought to be in London)

Portrait of two Women, about 1845
Daguerreotype, 8.7 × 6.7 cm

Wilson Centre for Photography, London (84:1193)

A similar combination of admiration and puzzlement shines through in the first three sentences of the piece in the 1843 *Illustrated London News:* 'A picture has just been added to the National Gallery which affords as much amusement to the public as it administers instruction to the colour-grinders, painters, and connoisseurs, who, since the day of its exhibition, have crowded the rooms to admire its singularity and discuss its merits. To every one it is a mystery. Its subject is unknown, its composition and preservation of its colours a lost art.'[12] The centuries-old challenge of determining the painting's subject thus continued, and for many years the official affordable catalogue of the National Gallery (priced at four pence) simply noted: 'The subject of this Picture has not been clearly ascertained.' Another more scholarly (and more expensive at one shilling) National Gallery publication set out to add knowledge based on the latest art-historical research, and can be seen as a forerunner of the present-day collection catalogues.[13]

While the fascination with van Eyck's verisimilitude endures, and questions remain to be answered, over the years the focus has shifted from the painting technique itself to the artist's virtuosity. Lorne Campbell has pointed this out most clearly, concluding that one of van Eyck's greatest achievements is not his 'realism' but, on the contrary, the 'art that conceals its artifice'.[14]

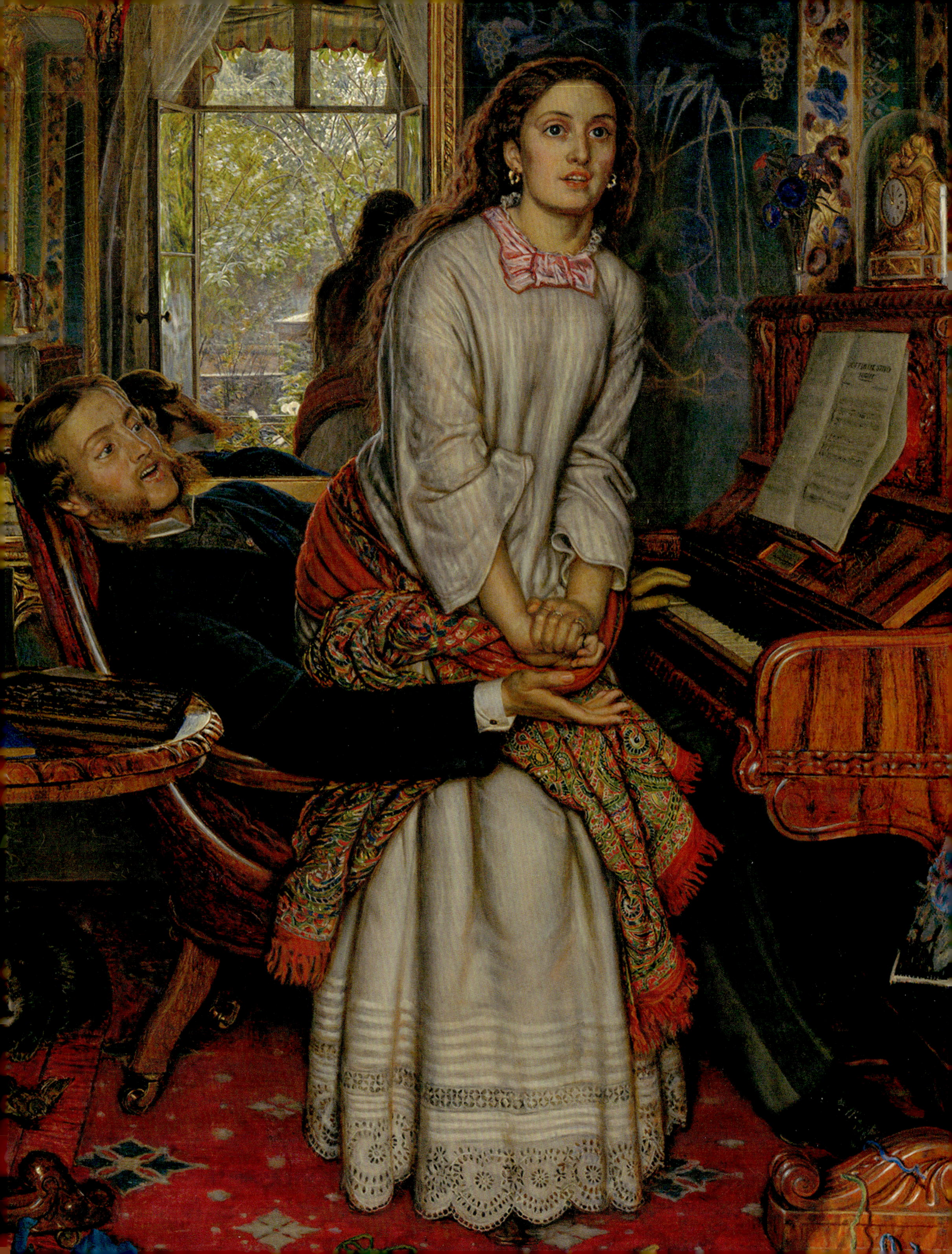

THE PRE-RAPHAELITE BROTHERHOOD

Caroline Bugler

Fig. 4
Detail of Cat. 18, page 42
William Holman Hunt (1827–1910)
The Awakening Conscience, 1853

In September 1848 three young students at the Royal Academy Schools – Dante Gabriel Rossetti, William Holman Hunt and John Everett Millais – banded together to form a radical new art movement. Disenchanted with what they saw as the sterile teaching they were receiving, they wanted to establish a new kind of painting with a fresh vision. While the Academy held up High Renaissance art as the pinnacle of achievement, the young artists found it unoriginal and bombastic. For them a more potent source of inspiration was earlier Italian and Netherlandish art of the fifteenth century, produced before the time of Raphael, which they admired for its purity and simplicity; they named their movement 'The Pre-Raphaelite Brotherhood' in a conscious act of homage. The word 'Brotherhood' intentionally suggested the idea of a medieval religious community or secret society, evoking the artists' appreciation of art and craftsmanship from the Middle Ages and their hope that they might revive religious art in the future.

The three artists soon added four further members to the group: the first of these was the sculptor Thomas Woolner (1825–1892), who shared their general dissatisfaction with the Academy. He was joined by Rossetti's brother, William Michael (1829–1910), a civil servant, amateur artist and critic; James Collinson (1825–1881), a fellow student at the Academy Schools, who was engaged to Rossetti's sister Christina; and Hunt's friend Frederic George Stephens (1827–1907), who became a chronicler of the movement. The group agreed to put the initials 'PRB' on their paintings while refusing to explain what they meant – a practice that inevitably gave rise to both puzzlement and jokes.

The Brotherhood was founded at a time of political and social turbulence – 1848 saw revolutions across Europe and a mass demonstration by the Chartists in England – and it shared something of the prevailing mood of radicalism.

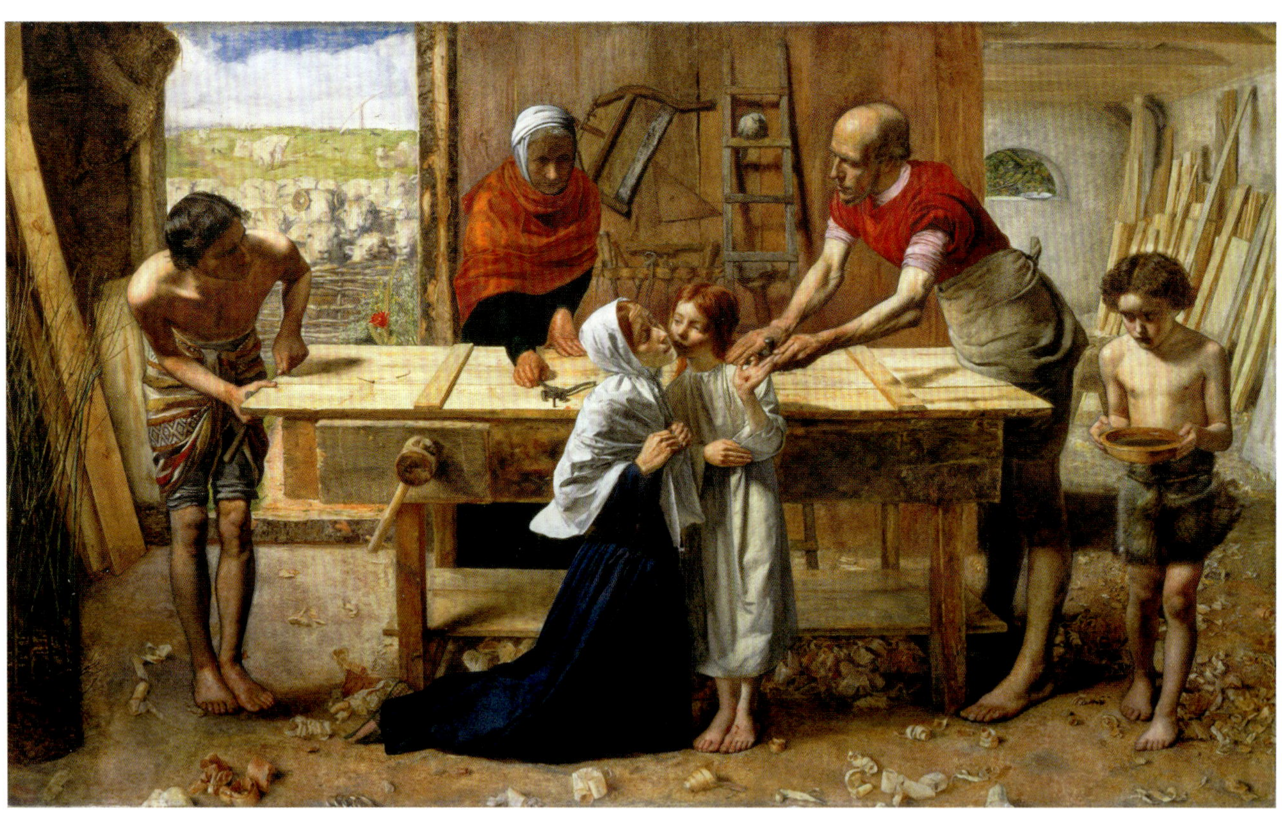

Fig. 5
John Everett Millais (1829–1896)
Christ in the House of His Parents (The Carpenter's Shop), 1849–50
Oil on canvas, 86.4 × 139.7 cm
Tate, London. Purchased with assistance from the Art Fund and various subscribers 1921 (N03584)

The artists never published a manifesto, but William Michael Rossetti later recorded the ambitions expressed at their initial meeting as: '1. To have genuine ideas to express; 2. to study Nature attentively, so as to know how to express them; 3. to sympathise with what is direct and serious and heartfelt in previous art, to the exclusion of what is conventional and self-parading and learned by rote; and 4. and most indispensable of all, to produce thoroughly good pictures and statues.'

While the artists professed admiration for pre-industrial medieval society they had a distinctly modern agenda. Their desire to express 'genuine ideas' meant abandoning the conventional scenes of military heroism and classical history that had formed a staple of Academic art, and anything they considered sentimental or frivolous, in favour of serious subjects with which they felt some direct emotional resonance. Their first works were religious, but they also chose themes from literature – Dante, Shakespeare, Tennyson and Keats were favourite authors – and medieval legend. They painted scenes of contemporary life too, including those that dealt with problematical social issues such as prostitution and poverty. Whether they were portraying historical or modern subjects, the young painters strove to depict physiognomy, costume and surroundings as accurately as possible.

Such exactitude could only arise from careful observation of nature, objects and people in the real world. Initially at least, this close study was conveyed in a hard-edged, sharp-focused style in which every detail was delineated with microscopic precision, and people were presented in unidealised form. Adopting a palette of brilliant, sometimes garish colour, the artists deliberately repudiated the chiaroscuro effects and conspicuous brushwork that they so disliked in the work of artists such as the Royal Academy's first president, Sir Joshua Reynolds (1723–1792), whom they nicknamed 'Sir Sloshua'.

The first pictures the Pre-Raphaelites exhibited attracted critical opprobrium for a variety of reasons including their perceived ugliness – Millais's *Christ in the House of his Parents* (fig. 5) was attacked by Dickens as 'mean, odious, revolting and repulsive'. But in 1851 the group found their greatest apologist, the critic John Ruskin (1819–1900), whose own views chimed with their aim of portraying nature as truthfully as possible. Their fortunes gradually improved, and they started to attract patrons, some of them newly rich industrialists from the north of England. They also began to gather artistic followers, including Walter Howell Deverell (1827–1854) and Arthur Hughes (1832–1915).

While the group was close-knit during its earliest years the individual inclinations of each artist soon began to assert themselves, and by 1853 the Brotherhood had effectively disbanded. Millais began to adopt a much looser style of working and went on to achieve great success, becoming a leading figure of the British art establishment and eventually president of the Royal Academy. Hunt attempted to remain true to the group's original aims, pursuing an art of high moral and religious seriousness. Rossetti initially abandoned oil painting in favour of detailed watercolours of medieval subjects, but from the 1860s specialised in luscious oil paintings of beautiful women inspired by Old Master paintings produced after the time of Raphael. These enshrined the concept of 'beauty for beauty's sake' and were antithetical to the chaste ideals and stark style of early Pre-Raphaelitism.

Such pictures marked the start of the second 'Aesthetic' phase of Pre-Raphaelitism, which was characterised by a dreamier, more introspective mood, and a distance from morally improving subject matter. Among the artists in Rossetti's extended circle were two younger adherents with whom he collaborated in a project to decorate the walls of the Oxford Union in 1857–9, Edward Burne-Jones and William Morris. Burne-Jones once declared: 'I mean by a picture a beautiful romantic dream of something that never was, never will be.' His work, which was shown in 1877 in the newly opened Grosvenor Gallery,

Fig. 6
Detail of Cat. 19, page 45
Ford Madox Brown (1821–1893)
'Take your Son, Sir!', begun 1851–2; enlarged and reworked 1856–7

to have considerable influence among younger artists in Britain and the Symbolists in Europe. He also collaborated with William Morris and others in extending Pre-Raphaelite ideals into the applied arts. Through his company, Morris, Marshall Faulkner & Co., which designed stained glass, textiles, furniture and wallpaper, Morris aimed to put into practice ideals of medieval, pre-industrial craftsmanship, and his work provided a cornerstone for the Arts and Crafts movement. Many women contributed to the venture, notably Morris's wife Jane and their daughter May, who were innovative designers and embroiderers.

While Pre-Raphaelitism had diversified and the artists had gone their separate ways well before the end of the nineteenth century, its influence continued to reverberate well into the twentieth century in the work of its followers and descendants.

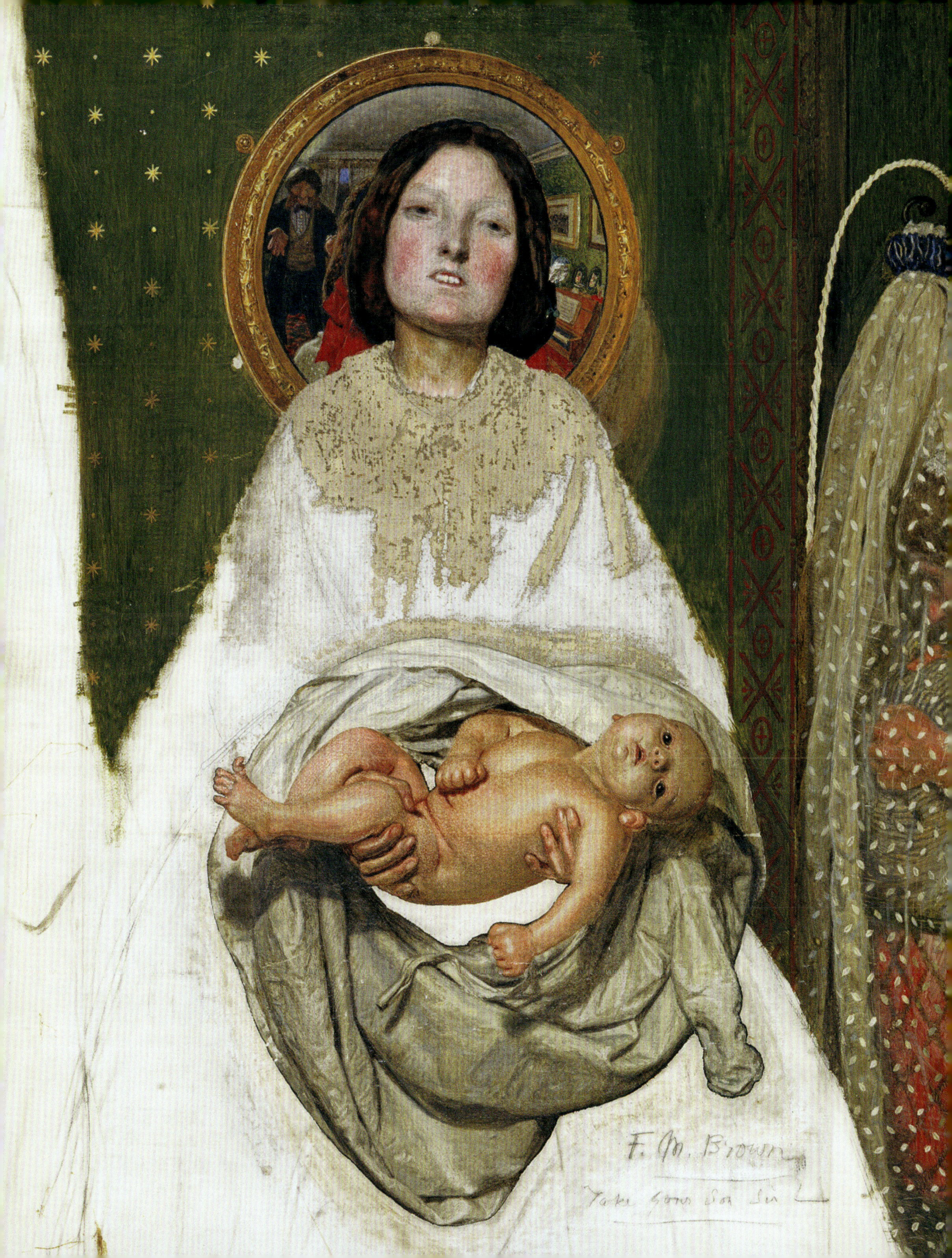
F. M. Brown
Take your Son Sir

THE PRE-RAPHAELITES AND THE ARNOLFINI PORTRAIT

A NEW VISUAL WORLD

Alison Smith

When it first went on display at the National Gallery in 1843, the *Arnolfini Portrait* was the only example of an early Netherlandish painting in the national collection. At a time when no standard history of the early Netherlandish school existed in the English language, this branch of art remained largely unknown and unappreciated, appealing mainly to antiquarians and revivalist painters such as William Dyce (1806–1864) and John Rogers Herbert (1810–1890).[1] As a high-resolution image in its minute and subtly illuminated rendition of forms arranged in a box-like interior, the portrait offered a new kind of realism not seen in the paintings on view at Trafalgar Square and rarely in the work of contemporary artists. The earliest direct response to it seems to have been Herbert's *Sir Thomas More and his Daughter* (fig. 7), exhibited the year after van Eyck's picture went on display at the Gallery, which also shows two figures depicted in minute detail standing together in a confined space, with More posed like Arnolfini.

In marked contrast to the idealisation that underpinned even the most naturalistic works on display at the National Gallery, including those by Dutch artists, van Eyck's distinct brand of realism chimed instead with the new aesthetic which photography was beginning to open up in Britain during the 1840s, the polished silver-plated copper surface of the daguerreotype mirroring the world with a similar forensic clarity. The picture's microscopic observation – which offered a parallel to the effects obtained with a camera – was frequently commented on.

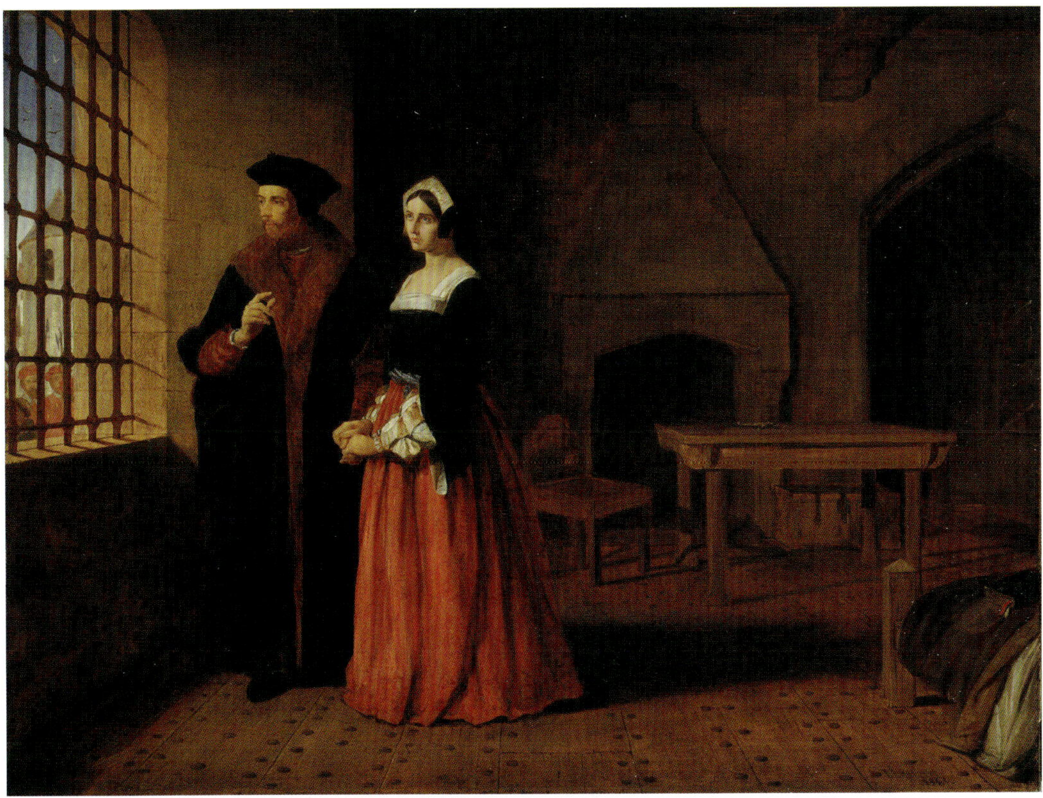

Fig. 7
John Rogers Herbert (1810–1890)
Sir Thomas More and his Daughter, 1844
Oil on canvas, 85 × 110.5 cm
Tate, London. Presented by Robert Vernon 1847 (N00425)

Nowhere was this connection felt more acutely than by the young artists who spearheaded the establishment of the Pre-Raphaelite Brotherhood in 1848. This movement was conceived in a spirit of reaction against what its founders derided as the formulaic and operatic art that followed in the wake of the High Renaissance and was upheld by the teachings of the Royal Academy. As students at the Academy schools, then housed in the east wing of the Wilkins building in Trafalgar Square, the three artists who led the movement – Dante Gabriel Rossetti, William Holman Hunt and John Everett Millais – had only to walk over to the west wing that housed the national collection to study the painting (fig. 8). It epitomised both the new modern idea of realism that lay at the heart of the group's ambitions, and the spiritual and creative integrity the artists perceived in the art of the Middle Ages, which prompted them to name their movement the Pre-Raphaelite Brotherhood.

The *Arnolfini Portrait* was special in that it was one of the few secular images to have survived from the fifteenth century, and it was certainly the most complex. By doubling up the interior space through the reflection in the mirror, the painting offered a view not just into a room but into a domestic realm transformed into something more mysterious. This was a picture that inspired the Pre-Raphaelites to look afresh at the everyday world and to present it as both real and strange.

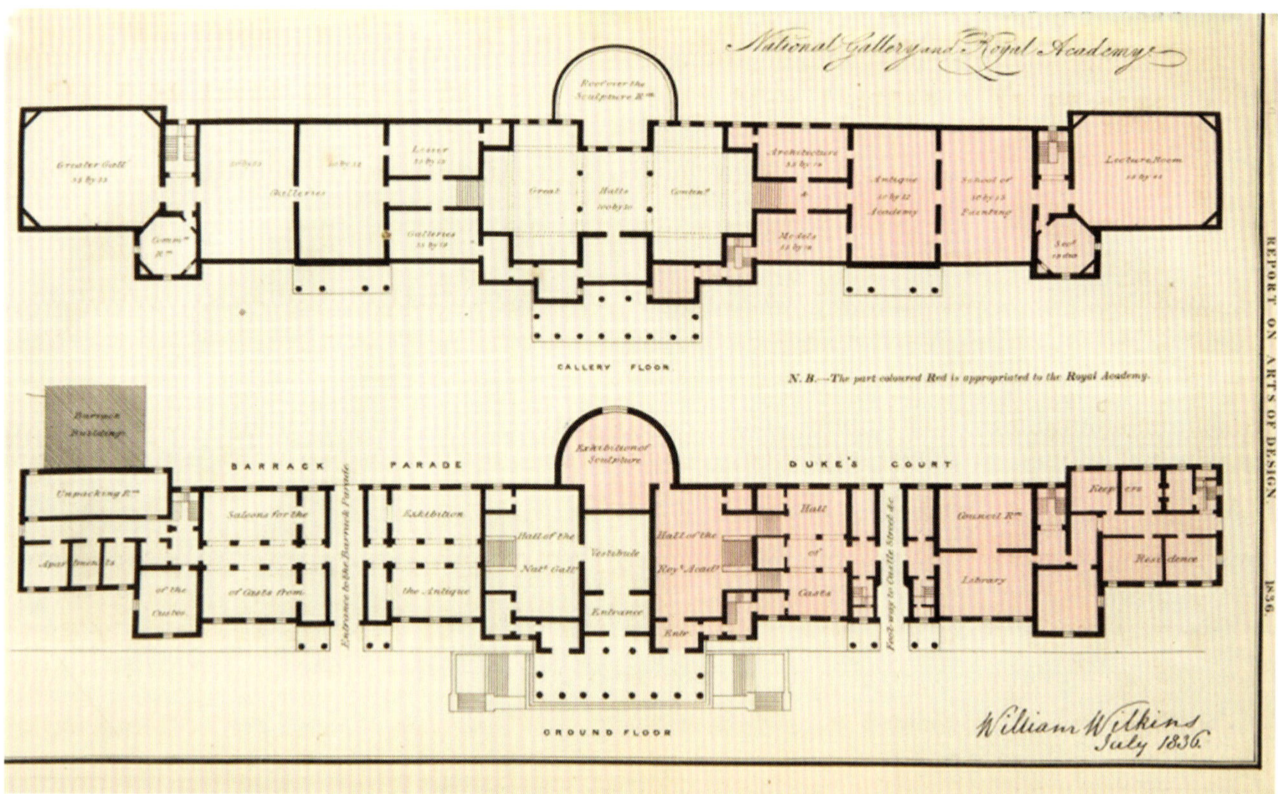

Fig. 8

The first floor and ground floor of the National Gallery and Royal Academy, by architect William Wilkins (1778–1839). Plan taken from the *Select Committee Report,* 1836. From 1837 until 1868 the Royal Academy was housed in the east wing of the building (shaded pink), allowing students access to the collections for study.

The National Gallery Archives, London

A similar combination of realism and fantasy can be found in literary creations such as Lewis Carroll's *Through the Looking-Glass* of 1871 and the poetry of Tennyson, whose sensory medievalism also influenced the style and subject matter of the artists' works.

While it is now accepted that the *Arnolfini Portrait* was an important catalyst in the development of the radical Pre-Raphaelite style, the artists themselves made very little written reference to it in the early years apart from F.G. Stephens, whose short story *The Reflection in Van Eyck's Mirror,* first published in 1856 in the American pro-Pre-Raphaelite journal *The Crayon,* may have been written as early as 1850.[2] Van Eyck's name does not appear in the 'List of Immortals' in the *Pre-Raphaelite Journal,* nor is he mentioned in the first accounts of the group's formation. Benozzo Gozzoli's frescoes at the Campo Santo in Pisa as interpreted by the engraver Carlo Lasinio, and the work of the German Nazarene painters based in Rome in the early nineteenth century, were held up instead as key exemplars.[3] In fact, at the time the young artists formed their Brotherhood it would seem that they had very little first-hand experience of Northern 'Pre-Raphaelite' art beyond the *Arnolfini Portrait,* the exception being their colleague and mentor, Ford Madox Brown, who had studied in Bruges, Ghent and Antwerp in the 1830s and must have been aware of the early Netherlandish painters. It is not known whether the artists ever attended the exhibition of Old Master paintings of early Northern and Italian art held in 1848 at the British Institution in London, and it was not until the end of the following year that Holman Hunt and Rossetti made a trip to Bruges, where they encountered further works by van Eyck and those by Memling (see pp. 19, 20–2 and 37).

The impression the *Arnolfini Portrait* made was explained only in retrospect, as some of the artists later acknowledged. Holman Hunt wrote in his memoirs of 1905 how he found sanction for his principles in 'the newly acquired Van Eyck', and Edward Burne-Jones recalled towards the end of his life: 'As a young man I have stood before that picture of the man and his wife, and made up my mind to do something as deep and rich in colour and as beautifully finished in painting.'[4] The artists' interrelated adaptations of van Eyck's work for their own historic and modern-life subjects would indicate that they were less interested in copying or imitating the *Arnolfini Portrait* than in initiating a kind of visual conversation around its distinct appearance and iconography. This dialogue resulted in some of the most extraordinary paintings associated with the movement, and established a pattern of influence that persisted well into the next century.

As part of their mission to emphasise the material presence of objects by recording them as faithfully as possible, the Pre-Raphaelites set out to produce 'thoroughly good pictures'. By this they meant durable ones, since the poor condition of many paintings in the national collection had become a matter of public debate.[5] In this context, the *Arnolfini Portrait* stood out as a picture still in immaculate condition, as the National Gallery's future director Charles Eastlake noted when he compared Vasari's observation that van Eyck's pictures were robust enough to withstand a vigorous wash with James Northcote's account of how a portrait by his master Sir Joshua Reynolds lost its face and neck when it accidentally overturned in the painter's studio. For the critic John Ruskin, the *Arnolfini Portrait* represented 'the highest reach of achievement with the strongest assurance of durability', amidst paintings in the National Gallery that were marred by 'blackened shadow and yellow light'.[6] Here there was a further link with photography, for the new reproductive processes were widely valued as a means of fixing and preserving the external world for future generations.

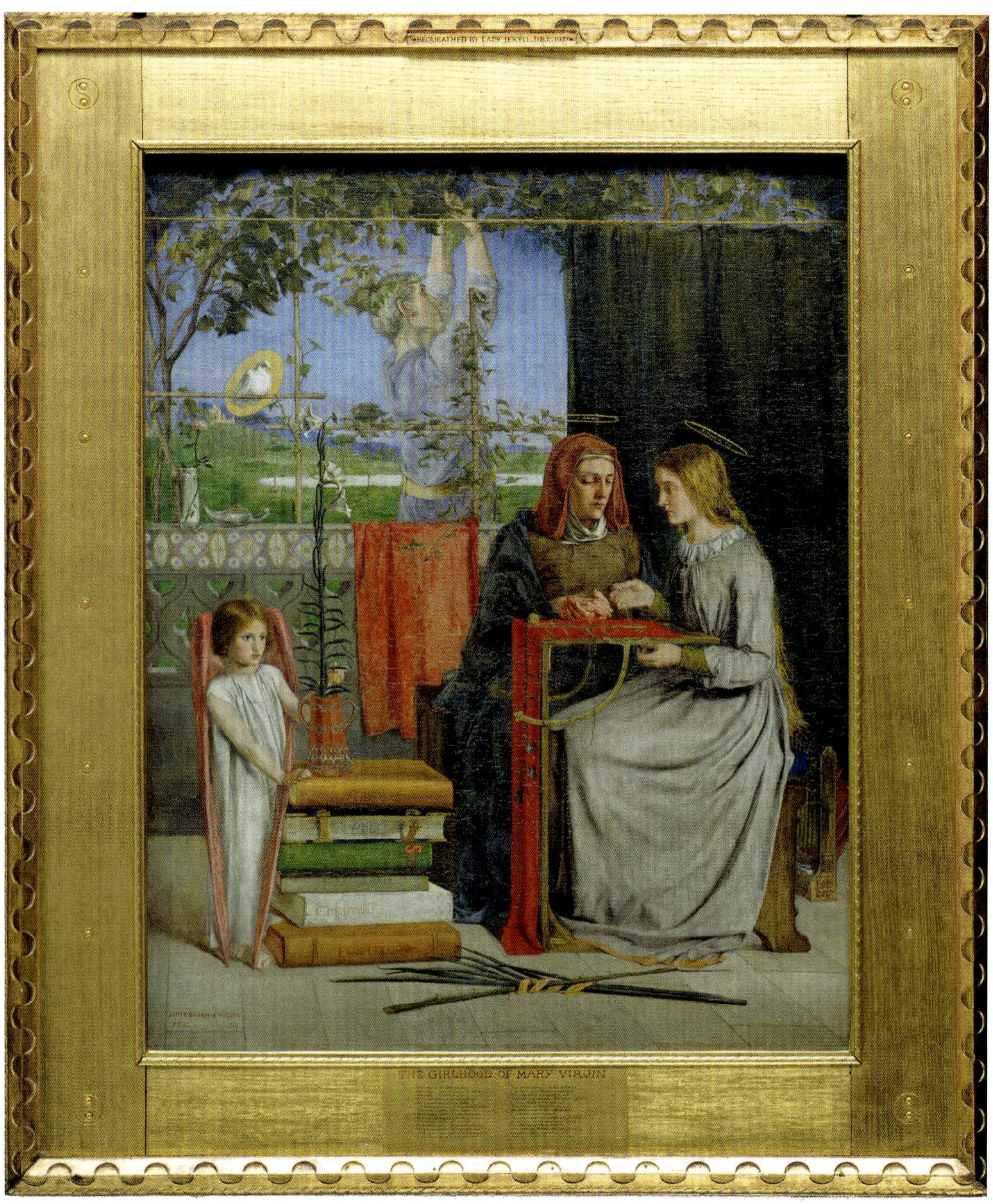

Cat. 13
Dante Gabriel Rossetti (1828–1882)
The Girlhood of Mary Virgin, 1848–9.
Oil on canvas, 83.2 × 63.4 cm
Tate, London. Bequeathed by Lady Jekyll 1937 (N04872)

In developing their own methods that built on earlier technical processes, and perhaps mindful of advances in the mechanical reproduction of images, the Pre-Raphaelites would have examined the *Arnolfini Portrait* at close range. They were also presumably aware of Eastlake's analysis of van Eyck's technique in the first volume of his *Materials for a History of Oil Painting* of 1847. As one of the earliest British texts to focus on the Netherlandish school, this emphasised the stability and resilience of its methods, characteristics Eastlake ascribed to the fixed nature of each preparatory stage. He also emphasised van Eyck's deployment of oil, and his use of a white ground to lend brilliance to his colour by reflecting light back through the transparent layers of paint – a system Eastlake believed may have been influenced by glass painting.[7] While they were certainly not interested in resurrecting lost processes with the intention of merely copying them, the Pre-Raphaelites did evolve a parallel system. This was based on the white ground upon which the design was drawn and then built up in transparent layers of paint in order to exploit the brightness of the underlying surface. To maintain the pitch of colour throughout a composition, they regularly employed a copal-based medium for binding their pigments, finding copal (a tree resin used for high-quality durable varnish) to be glossier on drying and capable of forming a clear layer in one application of the brush, creating an intense colour glaze, not unlike stained glass.[8] This type of method was applied in the first painting that appeared in public with the PRB initials: Rossetti's *The Girlhood of Mary Virgin,* exhibited at the National Institution's Free Exhibition of Modern Art in 1849 (cat. 13). Rossetti took great care over the execution of this picture: the artist William Bell Scott recalled that it was painted 'with watercolour brushes, as thinly as in watercolour, on canvas he had primed with white till the surface was as smooth as cardboard, and every tint remained transparent'. Indeed so smooth was the canvas surface that Rossetti's brother William erroneously described the picture as painted on panel.[9] By employing a painstaking technique which allowed each object to assume an almost tangible presence, Rossetti created a picture designed to invite symbolic interpretation in keeping with the words of the sonnet he pasted on to the frame. Although we can infer from Rossetti's itemisation of each object his close inspection of the *Arnolfini Portrait,* it is not altogether clear whether he would have regarded its details as part of some overall iconographic scheme, the actual meaning of the portrait being then (as it remains today) unclear.

In their compositional arrangements, the earliest Pre-Raphaelite paintings reveal an intense interest in van Eyck. More often than not, they show figures arranged tensely in interior spaces with an attention to detail not seen since the fifteenth century, reminding viewers of what had been lost following the High Renaissance. The departure from convention can be seen in Millais's portrait *Mrs James Wyatt Jr and her Daughter Sarah* (cat. 14), painted at the height of the group's notoriety. Here the facsimile reproductions of esteemed Old Masters on the wall (Raphael's *Madonna della Sedia* and *Alba Madonna,* and Leonardo's *Last Supper*) serve to highlight the real presence and unidealised depiction of the modern mother and child in the foreground. The rigidity of pose and lack of interaction echo that of the couple in

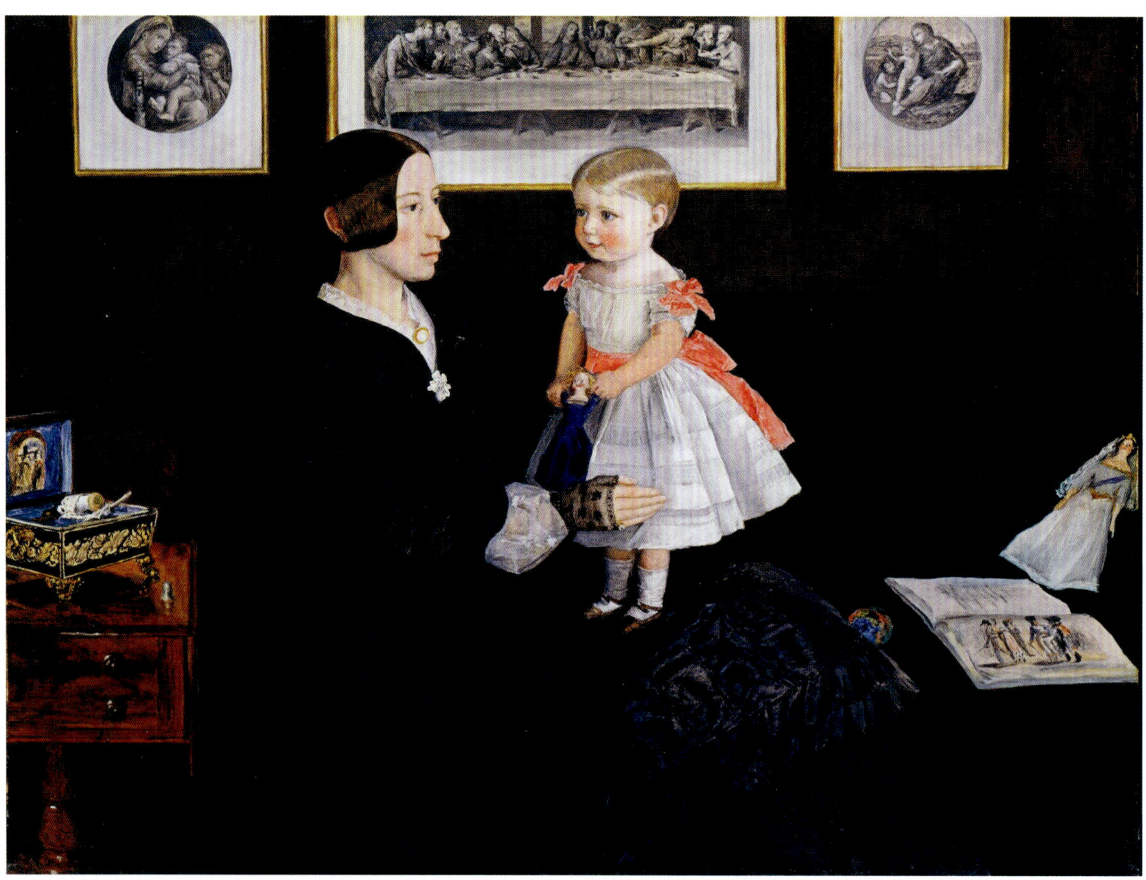

Cat. 14
John Everett Millais (1829–1896)
Mrs James Wyatt Jr and her Daughter Sarah, about 1850
Oil on mahogany panel, 35.3 × 45.7 cm
Tate, London. Purchased 1984 (T03858)

the *Arnolfini Portrait* and make the more graceful groupings in the prints appear artificial and mannered by comparison. As well as referencing actual 'Pre-Raphaelite' art, the arrangement of the figures also acknowledges the formalities of portrait photography, which required sitters to hold a pose and maintain a rather deadpan expression during exposure. A similar kind of presentation can be seen in the gold-toned daguerreotypes of Antoine Claudet, the foremost photographer working in London during the 1840s, whose portraits would have been familiar to the group (cat. 15). By equating the modern and commercial technology of photography with early Renaissance portraiture, Millais's painting doubles up as a manifesto for their shared authenticity, an authenticity that crucially admits the strangeness of perception that gave Pre-Raphaelitism its psychological edge and which in turn reflected back on van Eyck, inviting the human interest that has been one of the enduring attractions of his picture.

A number of works exhibited by the Pre-Raphaelites were certainly controversial. The dense layers of symbolism contained in pictures such as Millais's *Christ in the House of his Parents* (fig. 5, p. 26) and Hunt's *A Converted British Family* (Ashmolean, Oxford) exposed the group to accusations of being Tractarian or Roman Catholic sympathisers,

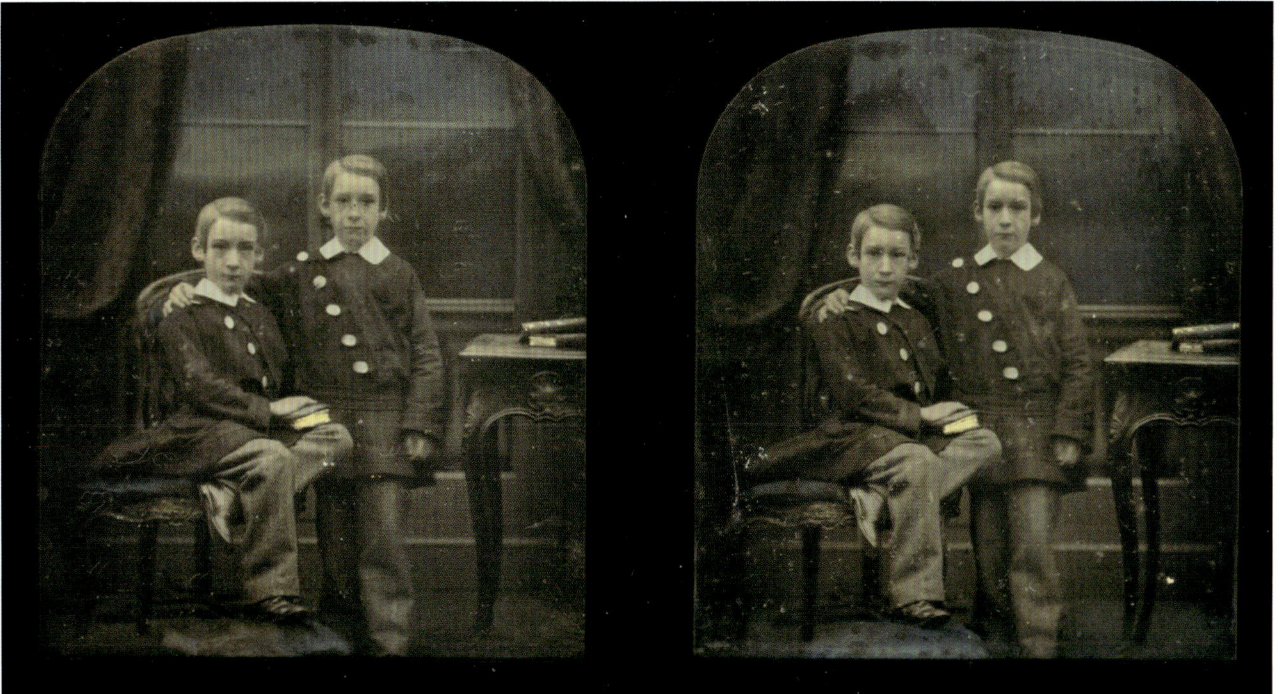

Cat. 15

Antoine Claudet (1797–1867)

Two Boys, thought to be Brothers, about 1855

Hand-tinted stereo daguerreotype, gold-toned, 6.7 × 5.7 cm

Wilson Centre for Photography, London (11:1312)

and the sharp linear realism of their style invited comparison with works by the so-called Northern Primitives. Respecting established taste, many critics of the day deemed the latter to be prosaic, hard and even grotesque compared to the early Italian masters. And in making the connection, some writers went so far as to suggest that the Pre-Raphaelites would be more appropriately titled 'pre-Van Eycks'.[10] By this it was implied that their works were ugly, breaching the boundaries of the rules of naturalism in art. The artists themselves certainly encouraged such an association. After Rossetti saw van Eyck's altarpiece in St Bavo's Cathedral in Ghent in 1849 he was inspired to re-think the traditional Annunciation theme in a work he titled *Ecce Ancilla Domini!* ('Behold the handmaid of the Lord', fig. 9), echoing the words van Eyck had inscribed beside his Virgin Annunciate. According to John Ruskin, Rossetti also intended to paint something 'like that van Eyck in the National Gallery with the man and woman and mirror' but failed to do so, although apparently he did attempt a troubadour scene of van Eyck in his studio.[11]

Millais did not have first-hand experience of the van Eycks and Memlings in Belgium, but his careful study of the National Gallery's van Eyck can be seen in the minute execution and glossy finish of his *Mariana* (cat. 16). Based on Tennyson's 1830 poem of the same name, this presents the character from Shakespeare's *Measure for Measure* alone in a moated grange having been abandoned by her fiancé, and longing for death. In contrast to the one-to-one equivalences favoured by Rossetti in cat. 13 (the lily standing for purity, for instance), the objects in *Mariana* function in a more

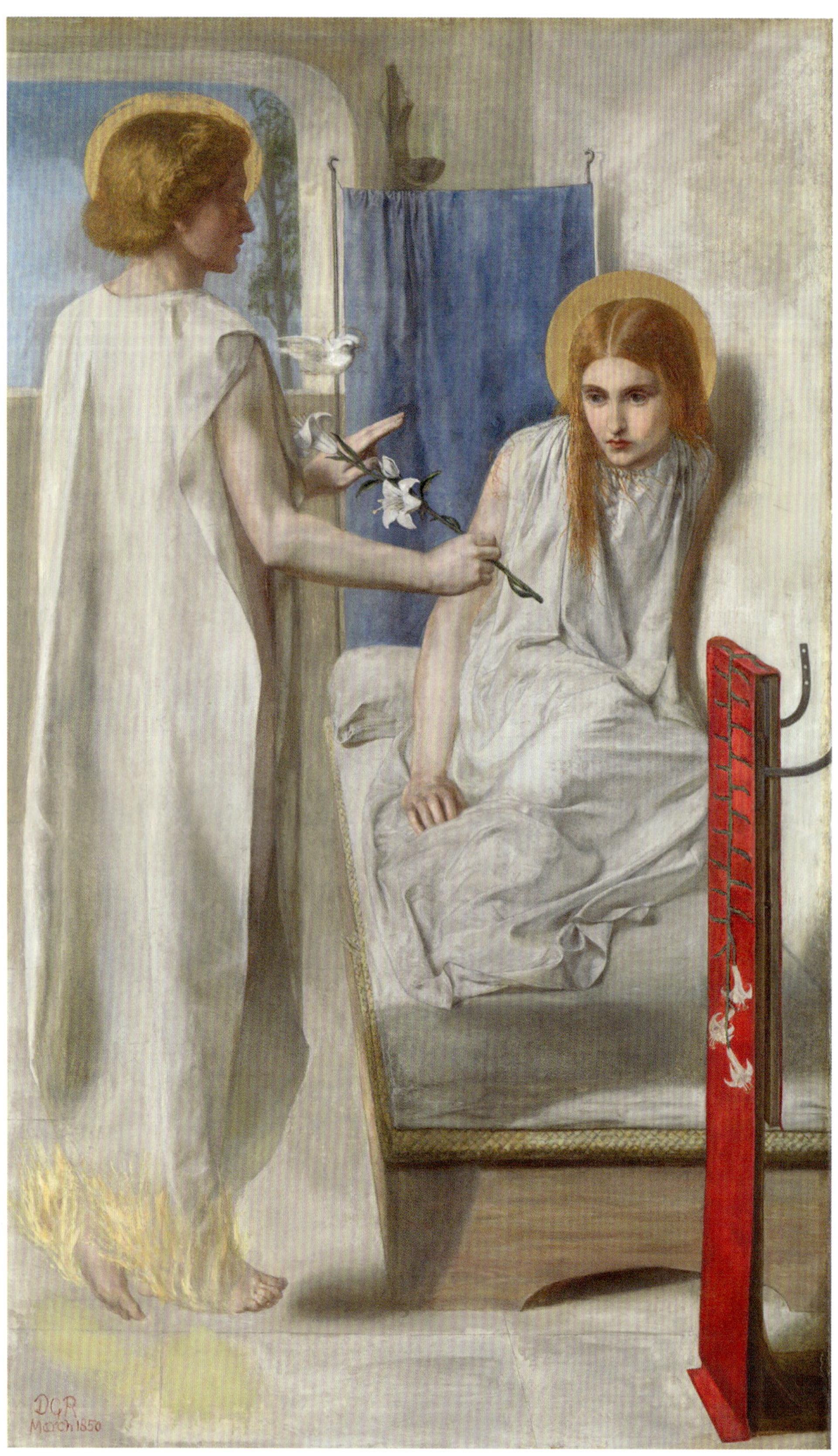
DGR
March 1850

Fig. 9
Dante Gabriel Rossetti (1828–1882)
Ecce Ancilla Domini! (The Annunciation), 1849–50
Oil on canvas, 72.4 × 41.9 cm
Tate, London. Purchased 1886 (N01210)

open way (as they do in the van Eyck), having a material presence of their own while also emphasising Mariana's conflicting feelings regarding her situation – the tension between her enforced seclusion and her yearning for love. The bed in the distance, the solitary flame and the appearance of a circular mirror in an early design (cat. 17, all citations from the *Arnolfini Portrait*), are suggestive of both the contemplative life and of physical desire. The pose of Mariana herself is the single most striking feature of the painting – the rich blue of her dress having Marian connotations while also accentuating the curvature of her figure in the same way that the bright green gown of the woman in van Eyck's painting exaggerates the swelling of her belly. The intimation here that Mariana could have been pregnant may have been prompted by the pregnancy theory raised in connection with the *Arnolfini Portrait* when it first appeared in public in 1841 (see pp. 13–14). The National Gallery's acquisition of van Eyck's *Portrait of a Man (Self Portrait?)* (cat. 2, p. 12) from the dealer Henry Farrer in 1851 would suggest a further level of engagement on Millais's part, as it was Farrer who purchased *Mariana* in advance of it being exhibited at the Royal Academy that year. The sale of the portrait may have encouraged Millais's interest in van Eyck, the carefully rendered (and deliberately unidealised) head of Mariana, with subtle transitions of tone revealing facial markings, inviting comparison with van Eyck's detached scrutiny of the head in his portrait.

By this time the Pre-Raphaelites had found a champion in Ruskin, who defended the movement on the basis of its moral realism, by which he meant the principle of 'absolute, uncompromising truth in all it does, obtained by working everything, down to the most minute detail, from nature, and from nature only'.[12] It was on similar terms that Pre-Raphaelitism was comprehended by French critics when some of the artists exhibited at the Exposition Universelle in Paris in 1855. Here the artists were praised for their humility and for an attention to detail comparable only to the early Netherlandish masters. Théophile Gautier described Millais as a painter who approached his subjects 'with the pious simplicity of Hemmeling [Memling], the glassy colour of Van Eyck, and the minute realism of Holbein'.[13] However, it was at the Art Treasures exhibition in Manchester in 1857, where the early Italian and Northern schools were hung on opposite walls, that the particularising realism of the latter really struck home, prompting a number of critics to draw comparison with the works of the Pre-Raphaelites shown elsewhere in the exhibition. This resulted in a more widespread identification of the early Netherlandish school as 'Pre-Raphaelite' and to the interpretation of van Eyck in particular as a modern realist painter.

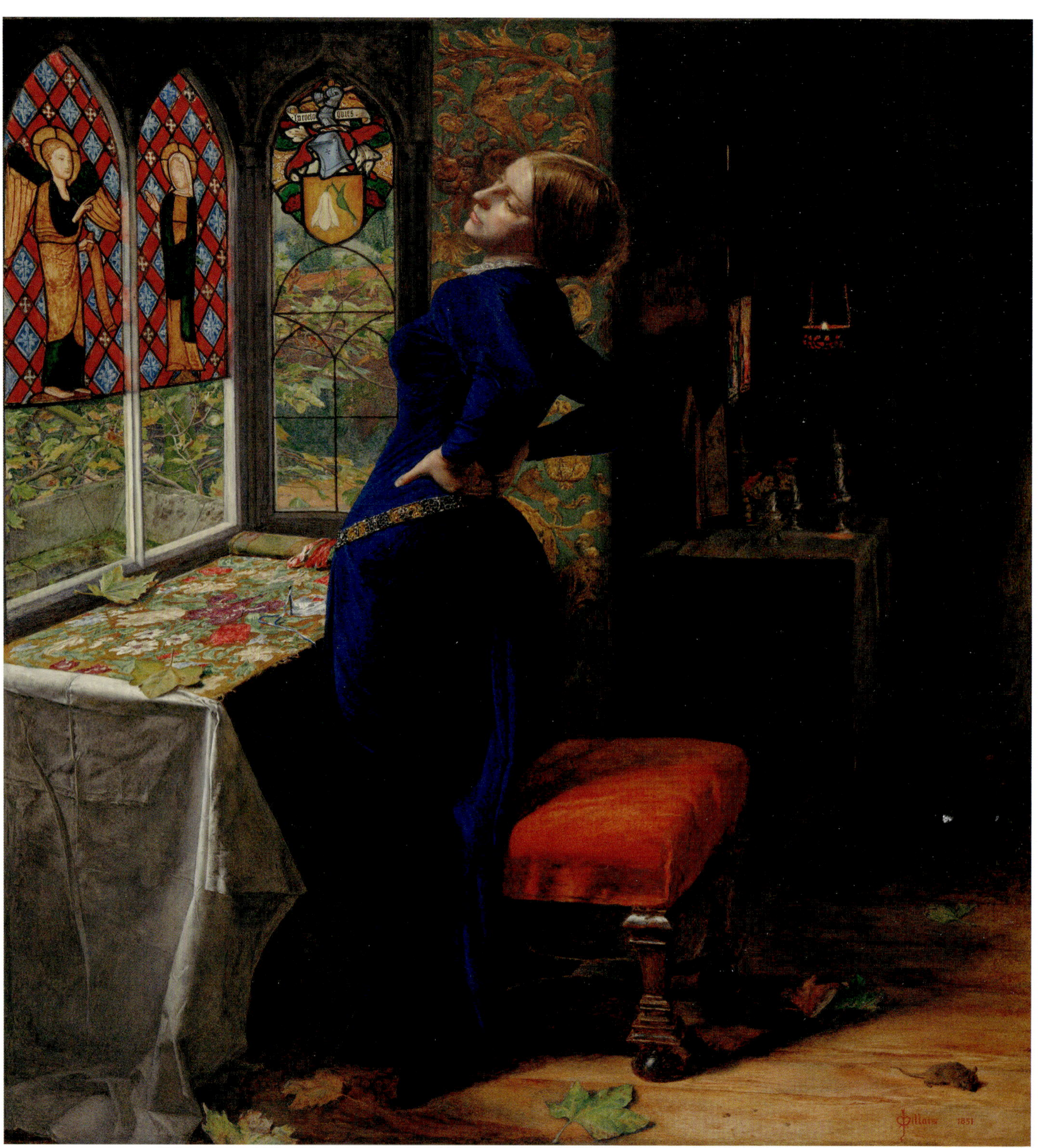
1851

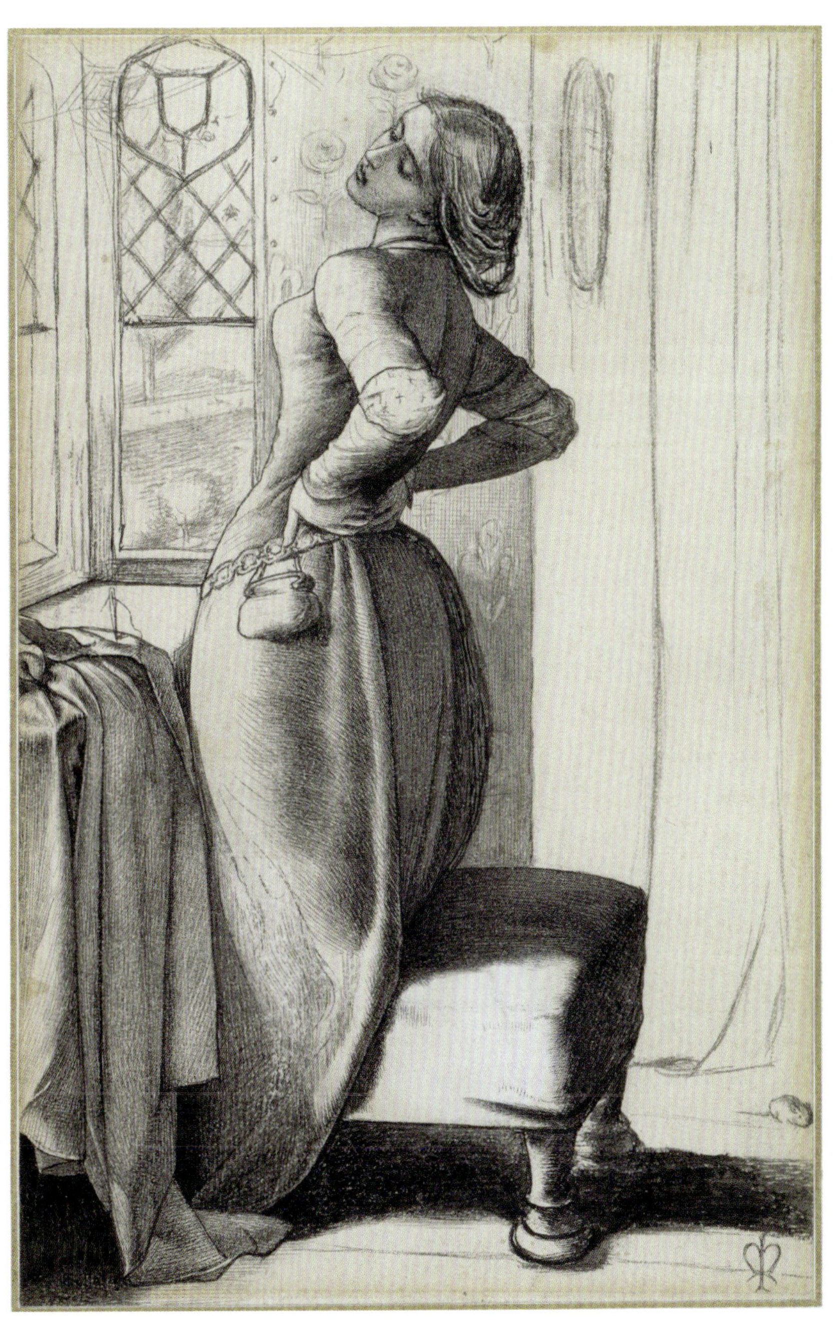

Cat. 16
John Everett Millais (1829–1896)
Mariana, 1851
Oil on mahogany, 59.7 × 49.5 cm
Tate, London. Accepted by HM Government in lieu of tax and allocated to the Tate Gallery 1999 (T07553)

Cat. 17
John Everett Millais (1829–1896)
Mariana in the Moated Grange, 1850
Pen and ink on paper, 21.5 × 12.9 cm
Victoria and Albert Museum, London (E.354-1931)

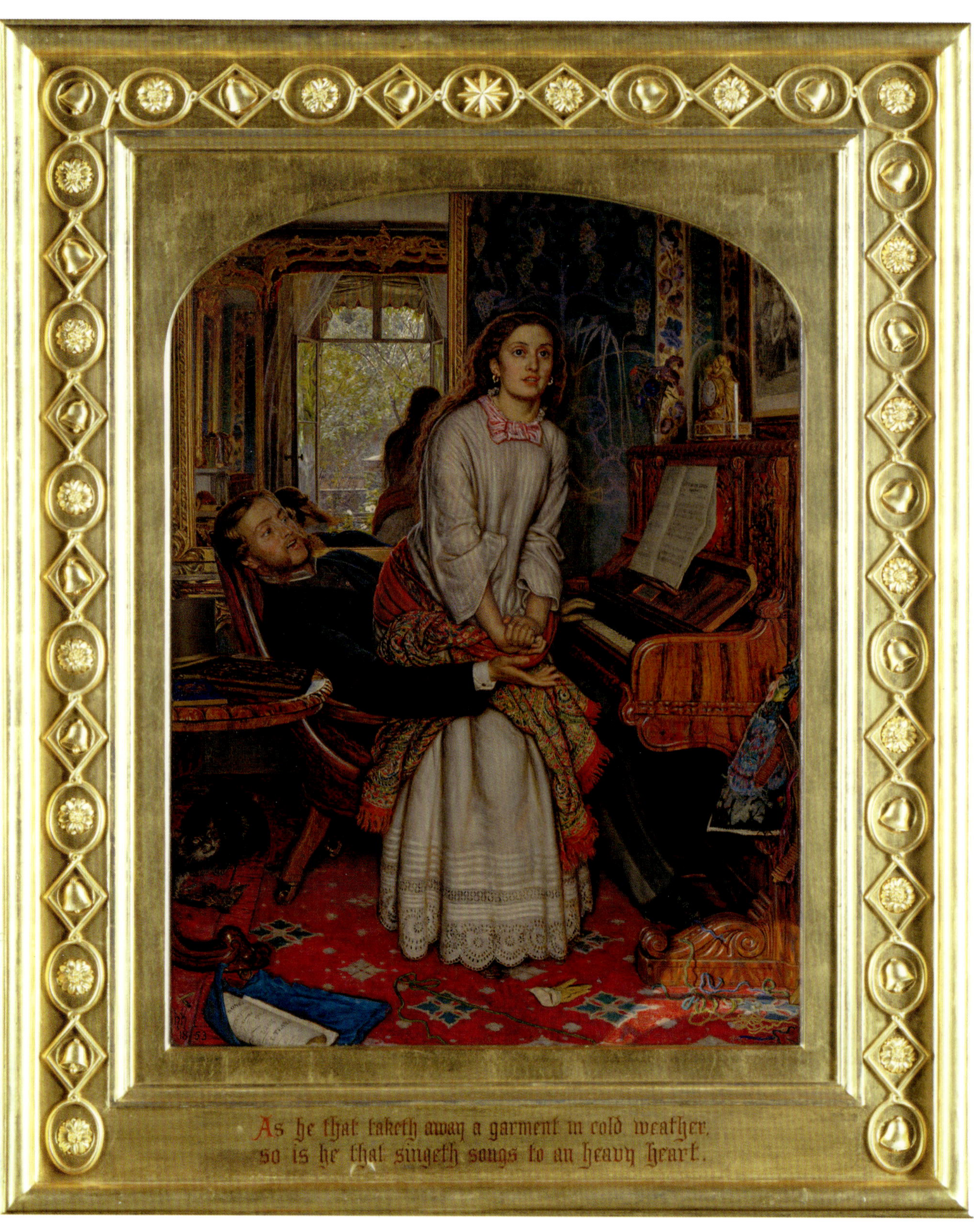
As he that taketh away a garment in cold weather,
so is he that singeth songs to an heavy heart.

THE CONVEX MIRROR

Cat. 18
William Holman Hunt (1827–1910)
The Awakening Conscience, 1853
Oil on canvas, 76.2 × 55.9 cm
Tate, London. Presented by Sir Colin and Lady Anderson through the Friends of the Tate Gallery 1976 (T02075)

Included among the recent British pictures at the 1857 *Art Treasures* exhibition was Holman Hunt's *The Awakening Conscience* (cat. 18), probably the most complex and influential of all the Pre-Raphaelite engagements with the *Arnolfini Portrait,* and certainly the first of their exhibited paintings to deploy a mirror to elicit a new metaphysical understanding of the modern everyday subject. The convex mirror placed like an eye at the centre of the *Arnolfini Portrait* was of special interest in this context, inviting comparison with the camera lens, the clear glass surface of which was enabling photographers to re-create the world. In van Eyck's day the circular, slightly curved surface was the only shape then available for glass mirrors, which were luxury objects. Manufactured in Venice and in northern Europe (the Bruges guild of painters included glass makers), they were backed with molten lead, the convex profile lending the mirror its distinct deforming characteristics by simultaneously expanding and compressing vision. The seemingly magical properties of the convex mirror had intrigued artists since the fifteenth century, encouraging van Eyck to capture subtleties of reflection, and later Parmigianino to explore the boundaries of truth and fiction in his celebrated *Self Portrait in a Convex Mirror* (fig. 11).

As the mirror became an established motif in Pre-Raphaelite art, artists employed their paint to present on canvas the virtual reality created by the reflective surface of what had then become a desirable item for the middle-class interior – a development abetted by technical advances in glass production and the 1845 repeal of the glass tax. Indeed the novelty of the mirror in the *Arnolfini Portrait* was such that it spawned the reproduction of replicas and small-scale circular mirrors for the modern home. While these were generally regarded as 'agreeable accessories' in much domestic advice literature of the time, the capacity of convex mirrors to confuse the viewer's sense of space and form encouraged the counter perception that these objects were somehow perverse in expressing in material form what design historian Juliet Kinchin has described as the sense of psychological suffocation and neurosis that Freud later identified as linked to the home.[14] The interior specialist Mary Eliza Haweis (who took over Rossetti's residence in Chelsea after his death in 1882) was wary of what she called the 'convex horror…wherein you see your brow or jaw swell sickeningly, your eye burst forth or your mouth protrude, according to the position in which you place your devoted head (fig. 10)'.[15]

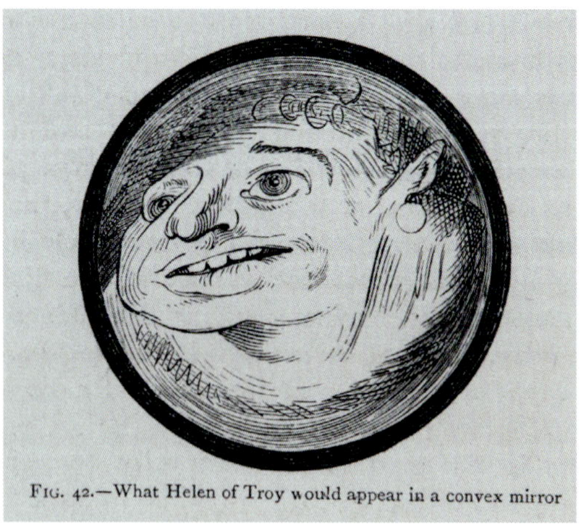

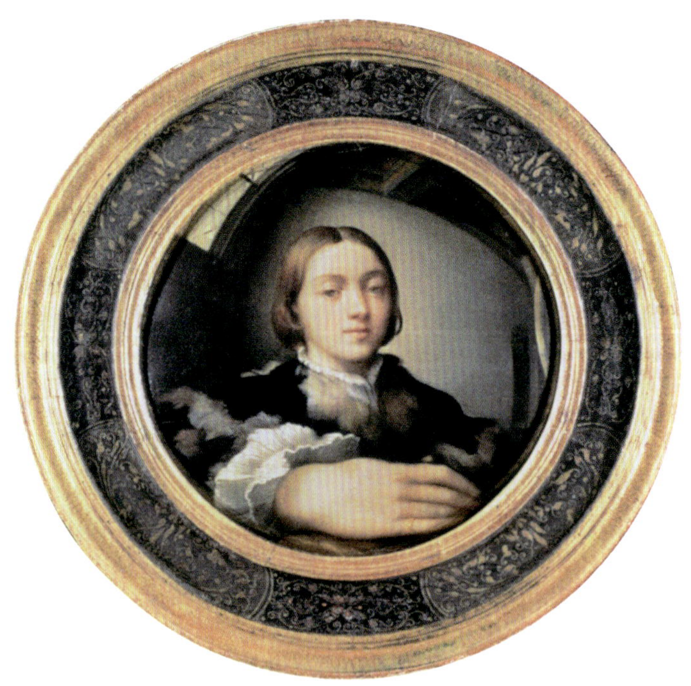

Fig. 10
'What Helen of Troy would appear in a convex mirror' from Mrs Haweis, *The Art of Decoration*, 1881

Fig. 11
Parmigianino (1503–1540)
Self Portrait in a Convex Mirror, about 1524
Oil on convex panel, 24.4 cm diameter
Kunsthistorisches Museum, Vienna

Cat. 19
Ford Madox Brown (1821–1893)
'Take your Son, Sir!', begun 1851–2; enlarged and reworked 1856–7
Oil on canvas, 70.5 × 38.1 cm
Tate, London. Presented by Miss Emily Sargent and Mrs Ormond in memory of their brother, John S. Sargent 1929 (N04429)

The appearance of mirrors in the modern bourgeois home and their implicit threat brings us back to Hunt's *Awakening Conscience*. Here the objects that clutter the room with their gaudy reflective surfaces provide the foil to the illicit relationship and double standard of sexual morality that forms the subject of the painting, itself a deliberate inversion of the harmonious marriage scene witnessed by van Eyck in his portrait. Set in the parlour of a fashionable villa in London, a wealthy gentleman is shown dallying with his mistress who, perhaps alerted by a chord he strikes on the piano, rises up from his lap and gazes out at a sun-infused garden which appears bright and fresh compared to the gloomy claustrophobic interior, suggesting an innocence she has lost and may never regain. Like the other items of furniture in the room, the mirror is large and flashy and indicative of an income as disposable as the woman is herself. It also allows the spectator to empathise with her plight and with what she feels and experiences within at her moment of epiphany. Emphasised as real, material presences, these objects take on a psychological significance, forcing themselves, in Ruskin's words, 'upon the disorganised mind of the woman'.[16] Here Hunt anticipates Panofsky's later reading of the *Arnolfini Portrait* in terms of a disguised or hidden symbolism disclosing deeper metaphysical truths (see p. 13). Each faithfully rendered object suggests a situation of vulnerability and entrapment, with the mirror opening up the possibility of redemption.

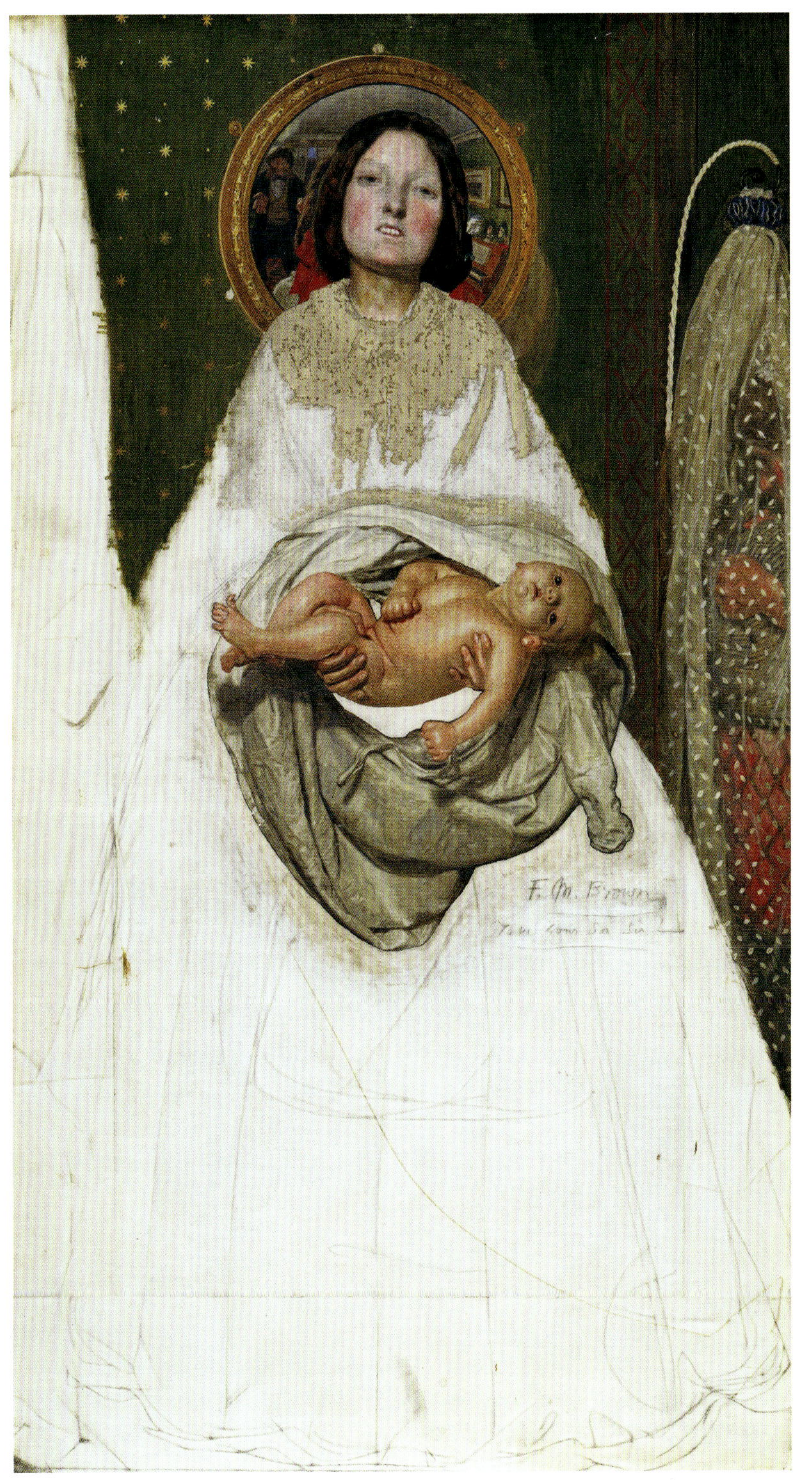

The conflation of secular and spiritual meaning in van Eyck's double portrait was adapted by Hunt for the symbolic realism he elaborated in the *Awakening Conscience* to probe the moral conflicts underpinning modern relationships. This concern was partly driven by the artist's own complicated entanglement with the working-class model Annie Miller, who posed for the figure of the kept woman, and whom Hunt intended to marry after educating her for her future role as his wife. In this he may have been aware of the picture Ford Madox Brown started in 1851 (cat. 19), which also references the *Arnolfini Portrait* in presenting a modern domestic situation. Inscribed 'Take your Son, Sir', the unfinished painting includes, at its optical centre, a small contemporary convex mirror suggestive of a family of more modest means than the household depicted in Hunt's work. Presumably aware of the different theories in circulation about the original intended significance of the *Arnolfini Portrait* – whether it was an actual portrait of van Eyck and his wife, or of a couple who had conceived a child outside of marriage (see pp. 13–14) – Brown set out to present a narrative that was equally suggestive and which involved, as its protagonists, his mistress and (from 1853) wife, Emma; his third child, Arthur Gabriel;

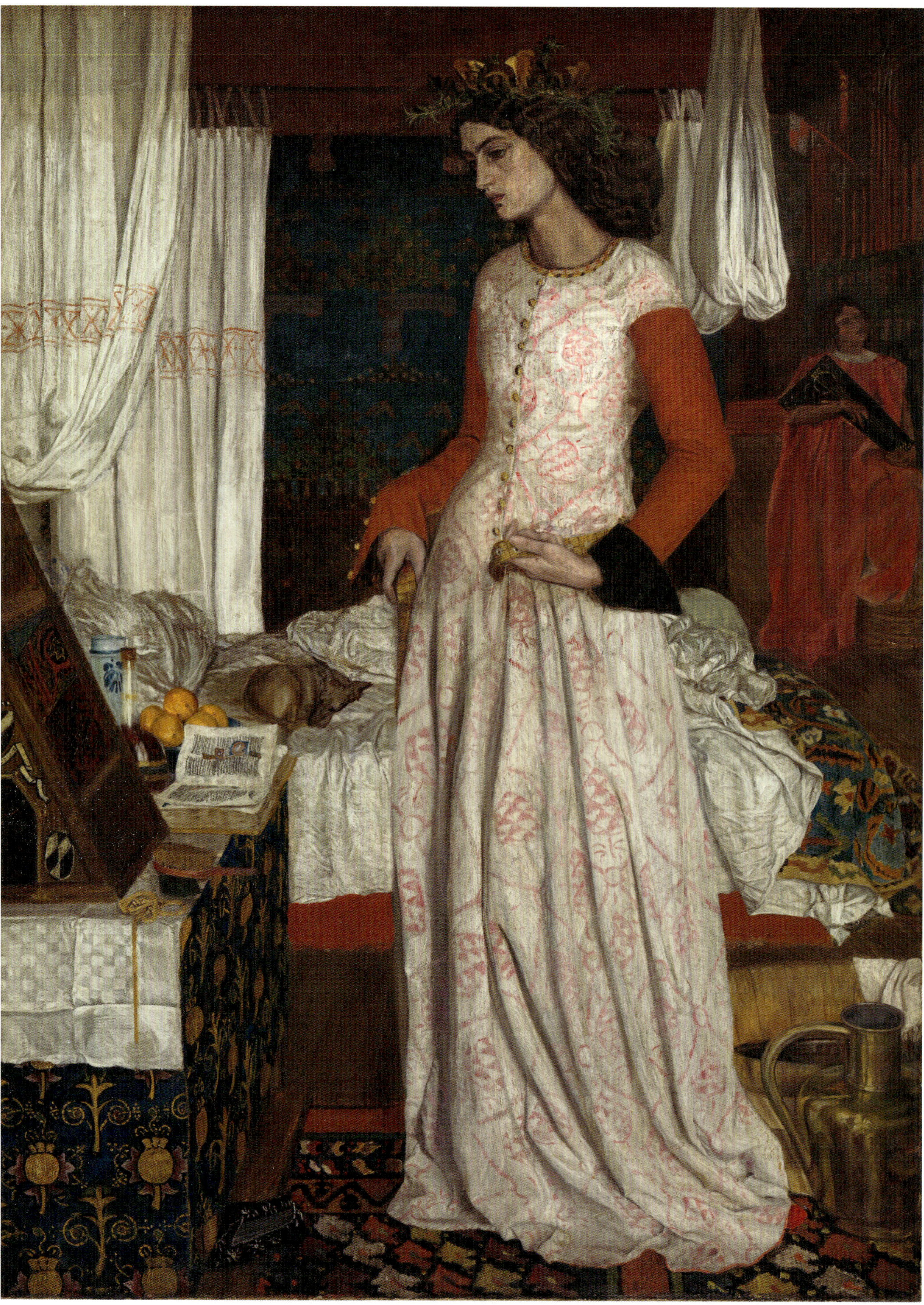

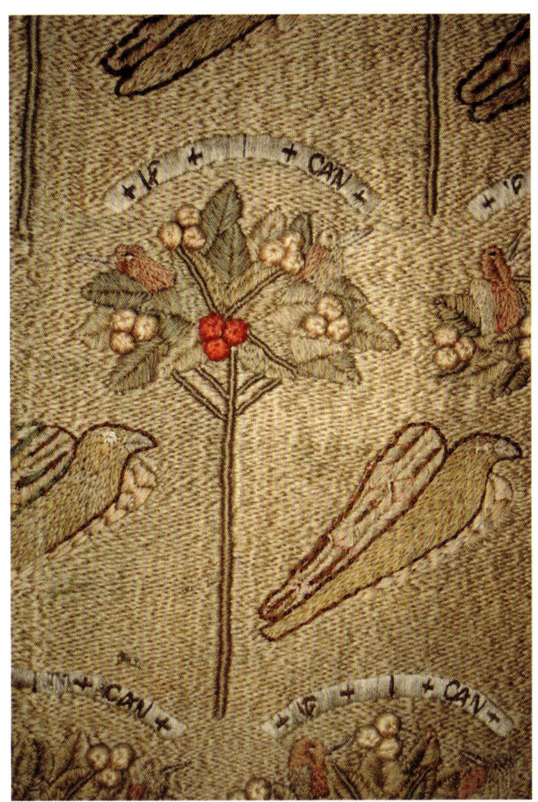

Fig. 12
William Morris (1834–1896)
If I Can, 1847
Embroidery on wall hanging
Kelmscott Manor

Cat. 20
William Morris (1834–1896)
La Belle Iseult, 1857–8
Oil on canvas, 71.8 × 50.2 cm
Tate, London. Bequeathed by Miss May Morris 1939 (N04999)

and himself depicted on Lilliputian scale reflected in the convex mirror. While the format and colour scheme evoke the serene domestic scene celebrated in van Eyck's portrait, the words uttered by the woman as she holds out the child to the man would appear to hint at a more tense moment, giving rise to suggestions that the painting was intended to address the theme of illegitimacy, or what the first director of the Tate, Charles Aitkin, more politely termed 'a tragedy of bourgeois domestic married life'.[17] The anamorphic distortion provided by the mirror exaggerates the gesture of the man as he holds out his hands to receive the child from the seemingly exhausted woman; at the same time it offers a view into what appears to be a cosy lower-middle-class interior, complete with piano, a glass-covered clock and framed prints. By confusing audience perception Brown makes it difficult for the viewer to ascertain whether the couple are just preparing the baby for bed or partaking in a more fraught discussion about its future.

The *Arnolfini Portrait* thus came to inform Pre-Raphaelite practice in two interconnecting ways. Its precise rendition of nature influenced the artists' treatment of the visible world, while the imaginary realms opened up through the mirrored reflection suggested an alternative reality. William Morris's *La Belle Iseult* (cat. 20) is a picture that pays homage to Eyckian fact as if to mask over the personal ramifications of the subject. Using his future wife (and Rossetti's future lover) Jane Burden as model, and basing the picture on Malory's version of the Tristram and Iseult legend, Morris shows the princess forlorn in her chamber, mourning her lover's absence following his exile from her husband King Mark's court. Here the Arthurian legend justifies the representation of adultery – a theme that was as morally problematic in contemporary society as Hunt's subject of prostitution. The bed, carpet, oranges, dog, mirror and slipper have all been transposed from van Eyck; likewise the pose of Iseult and the sheer perspective of the floor. While these features serve symbolically to accentuate Iseult's sense of isolation, Morris's other point of interest seems to lie in the existence of the objects as real decorative items similar to those he was already producing and was soon to specialise in making with the establishment of the design collective Morris, Marshall,

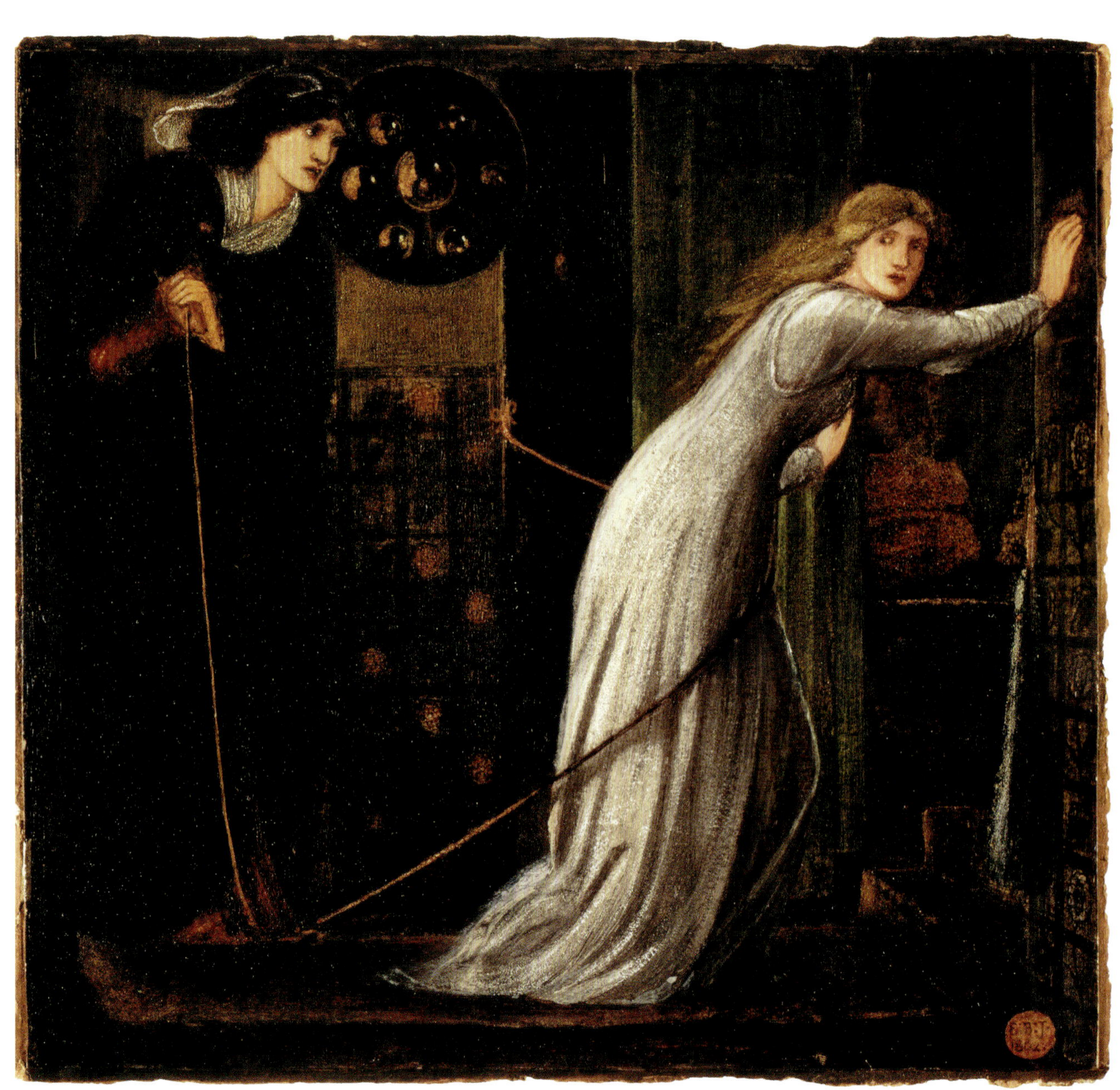

Cat. 21

Edward Burne-Jones (1833–1898)

Fair Rosamund and Queen Eleanor, 1862

Ink, watercolour, gouache and gum on paper, 26 × 27.3 cm

Tate, London. Presented by J.R. Holliday through the Art Fund 1923 (N03822)

Faulkner & Co. in 1861. It was around the time Morris embarked on this picture that he adopted as his personal motto the words *Als Ich Kan* (which he interpreted as 'If I can' but are now translated as 'As I can') that van Eyck had inscribed on the frame of the *Portrait of a Man* in the National Gallery (cat. 2, p. 12). This inscription first appears in a wall hanging of roughly the same date at Kelmscott Manor (fig. 12) which is very similar to the blue stitched tapestry in the background of the painting, and came to stand for Morris's belief in the beauty and usefulness of hand-crafted objects as epitomised by the workmanship of the Middle Ages.

A similar concern to apply Eyckian vision to the actual crafting of objects can be seen in the work of Morris's close friend, Edward Burne-Jones. Like Morris and Hunt, Burne-Jones was fascinated by the central mirror, but not so much as a medieval accessory or for enhancing pictorial illusionism, as for how it might disclose hidden designs or dark magic. Much of the artist's early work was based on legends involving unnatural family relationships which comprised a kind of domestic grotesque, one example being the small painting based on the legend of Fair Rosamund and Queen Eleanor (cat. 21). Here the mirrored discs that surround the convex mirror pick up different facets of the Queen's profile as she ensnares her victim with the cord she has followed to find Rosamund in her hidden chamber. A study for the mirror (cat. 22) shows how closely the artist attended to the kaleidoscopic pattern of revolving heads in order to dramatise the sinister intentions of the Queen. According to the artist's wife, Georgiana, this was based on a mirror specially constructed for the subject by Burne-Jones's father, a frame-maker, but the measurements of the spaces proved to be faulty, destroying the design.[18]

Burne-Jones's appropriation of the convex mirror for purposes of distortion and divination parallels the work of Rossetti, who around the same time started to depict legendarily evil women. In *Lucrezia Borgia* (cat. 24), the eponymous instigator of her husband's death is shown cleansing her hands after administering poison. Reflected in the mirror, the husband hobbles on crutches assisted by Lucrezia's father and accomplice, Pope Alexander VI, 'to settle the poison well into the system'.[19] A comparable large convex mirror dominates Burne-Jones's van Eyck-inspired composition study for *St Valentine's Day* (cat. 23), its surface reflecting a maid preparing a wedding breakfast as Love enters the room to herald the dawn. In the (lost) finished watercolour, the mirror and window have exchanged places but the overall effect is to compress and extend space in order to disorient the viewer and heighten the dreamlike dimension of domestic space as an alternative to Pre-Raphaelite realism.

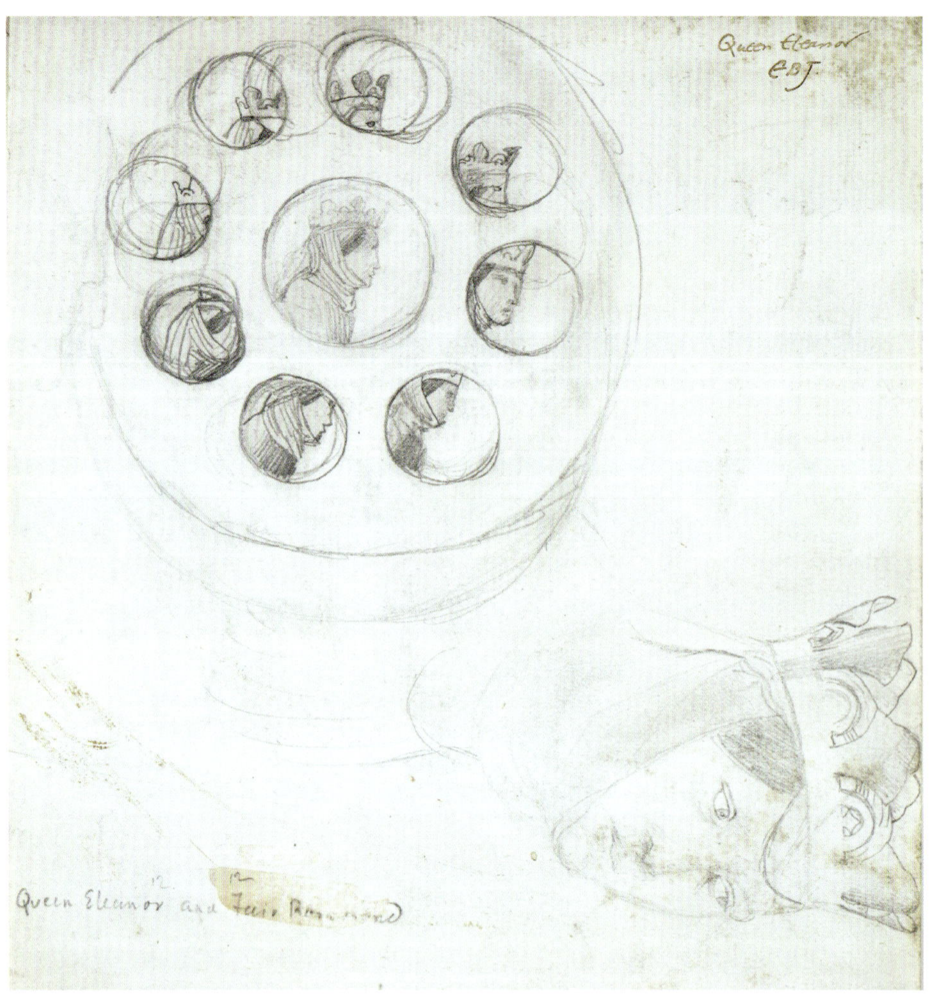

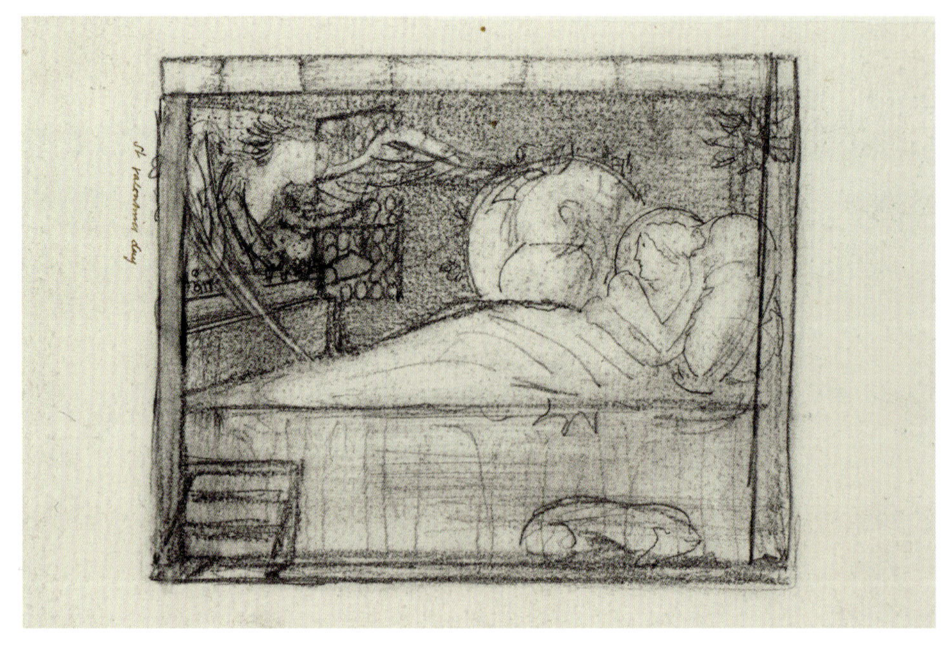

Cat. 22

Edward Burne-Jones (1833–1898)

One of seven studies for Queen Eleanor and Fair Rosamund, 1862

Pencil on paper, 24.6 × 22 cm

Victoria and Albert Museum, London. Bequeathed by J.R. Holliday (E.2857-1927)

Cat. 23

Edward Burne-Jones (1833–1898)

Study for St Valentine's Day, verso of Study for 'The Merciful Knight', about 1863

Graphite on paper, 25.8 × 17.8 cm

Tate, London. Bequeathed by J.R. Holliday 1927 (A00084)

Cat. 24

Dante Gabriel Rossetti (1828–1882)

Lucrezia Borgia, 1860–1

Graphite and watercolour on paper, 43.8 × 25.8 cm

Tate, London. Presented in memory of Henry Michael Field by Charles Ricketts through the Art Fund 1916 (N03063)

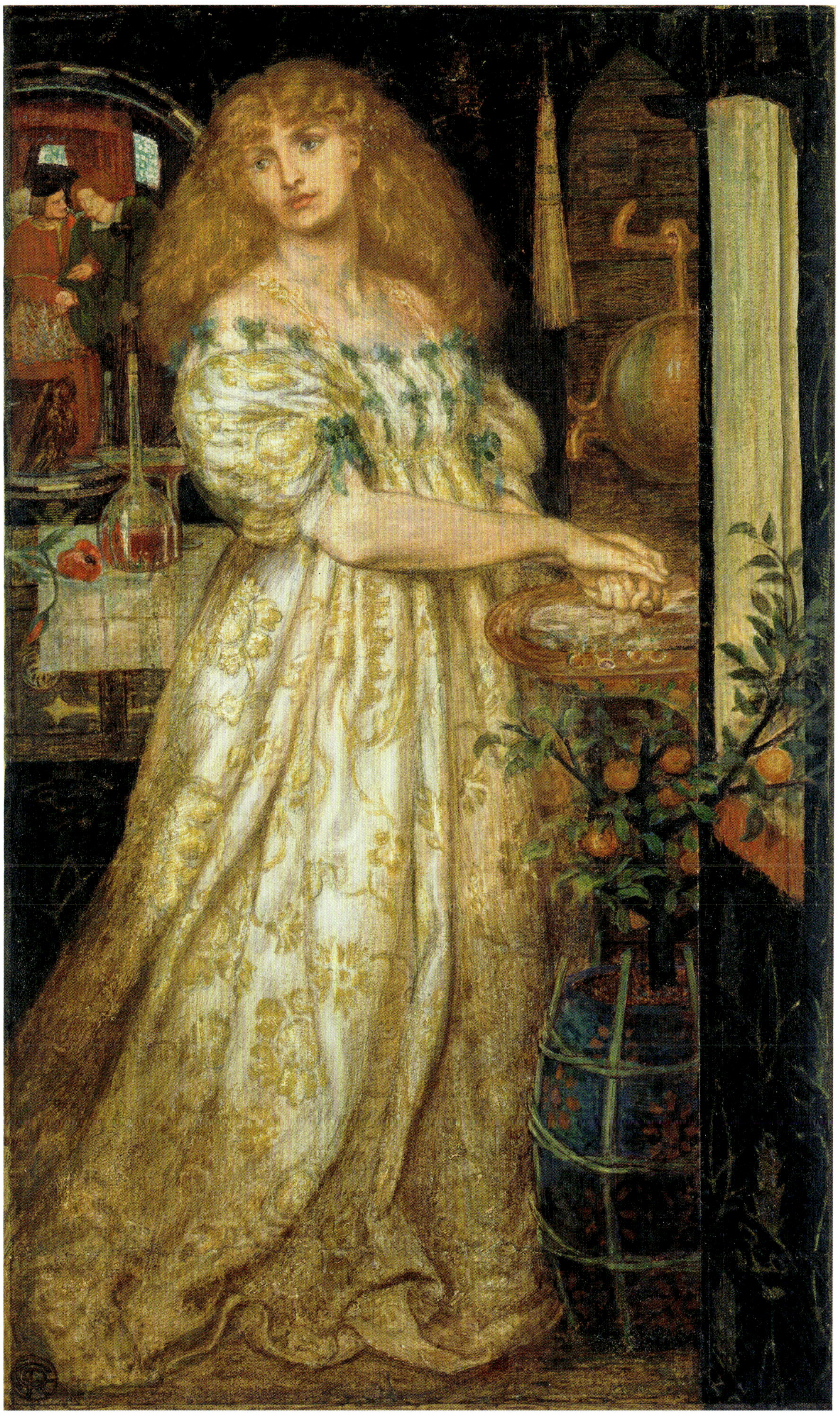

THE AESTHETIC MIRROR

Cat. 25
Simeon Solomon (1840–1905)
A Youth relating Tales to Ladies, 1870
Oil on canvas, 35.5 × 53.4 cm
Tate, London. Presented by the Kretschmer family in accordance with the wishes of William Kretchmer 1983 (T03702)

Cat. 26
Convex mirror owned by Dante Gabriel Rossetti (1828–1882)
32.7 diameter × 4.8 cm
Society of Antiquaries of London, (Kelmscott Manor, KM 611)

Cat. 27
Henry Treffry Dunn (1838–1899)
Dante Gabriel Rossetti's Bedroom at Tudor House, 16 Cheyne Walk, 1872
Watercolour on paper, 33.5 cm diameter
Wightwick Manor, the National Trust. Given to the National Trust by Mrs Helen Annie Handford Guglielmini in 2001 (1287978)

As an object that created strange hallucinatory effects, the convex mirror soon came to be associated with the Aesthetic interior, its appearance in paintings complementing the appearance of small-scale circular mirrors in the homes of the most advanced taste-makers of the day. The Aesthetic movement, which grew out of Pre-Raphaelitism, flourished in Britain in the 1870s and 1880s. Some artists, notably Rossetti and his followers, bridged the two movements, but in many ways the Aesthetic philosophy of 'Art for Art's sake' was antithetical to the principles that lay behind early Pre-Raphaelite works in its prioritisation of visual and decorative qualities over moral and narrative considerations. It also signalled a shift towards a more subjective mood in painting, and for many of the artists associated with the Aesthetic movement, including Rossetti (who had 24 mirrors in his Chelsea home, nine of which were convex), mirrors provided the link between the imaginative world of the painting and the internal world of the artist (cat. 26; fig. 13).[20] A defence perhaps against objective realism, the convex mirror assisted Rossetti in his mission to uphold an aesthetic that refracted prosaic reality into something more private and mysterious. The shift towards painting in a more suggestive way among artists in the Rossetti circle allowed them to underscore the unreality of images. Thus, in Simeon Solomon's *A Youth relating Tales to Ladies* (cat. 25), the small convex mirror on the wall reflects the murky shapes of what appears to be an easel and canvas, but no artist is shown witnessing the storytelling in the foreground, an absence that would seem to indicate a response as interiorised and unconnected as the reflection itself. The idea of the modern Aesthetic interior as a space for indulging private fantasy and reverie is similarly conveyed in the watercolour made by Rossetti's assistant, Henry Treffry Dunn, of the artist's bedroom at Cheyne Walk (cat. 27). Here the painting itself assumes the form of a convex mirror, exaggerating the bulging contours of the bed curtains to capture something of the enclosed introspective nature of Rossetti's lifestyle and the swelling limbs of the ideal female portraits for which he became well known. Burne-Jones's residence, The Grange in Fulham, featured similar mirrors which contributed to what the painter and collector Graham Robertson described as the 'tinted gloom' of the rooms 'through which clear spots of colour shone jewel-like', reflecting the refined melancholy nature of the artist's own romantic vision.[21]

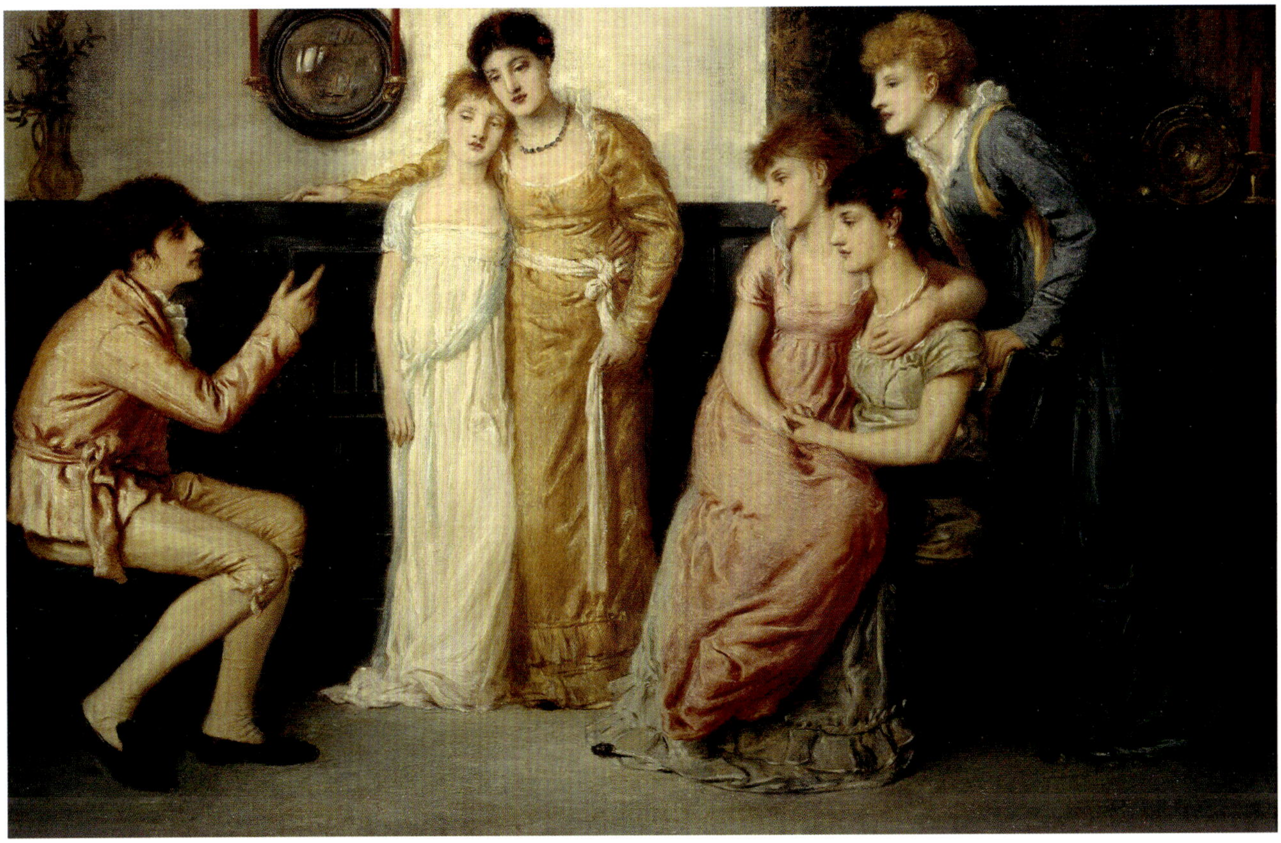

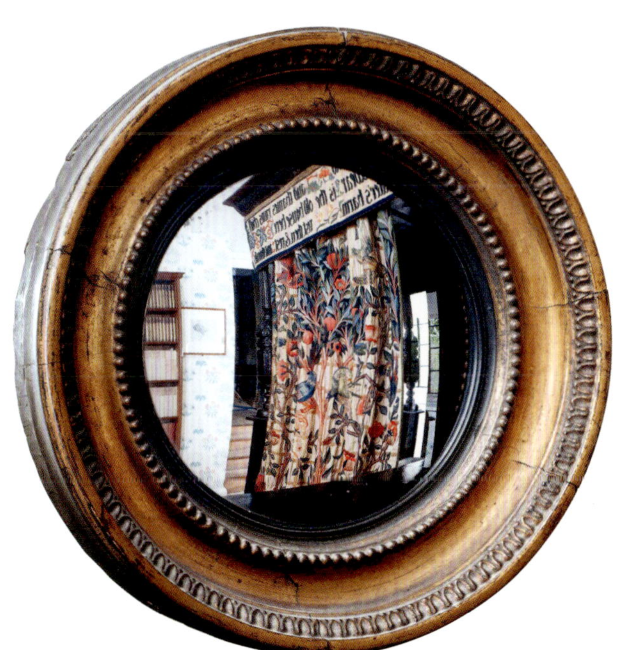

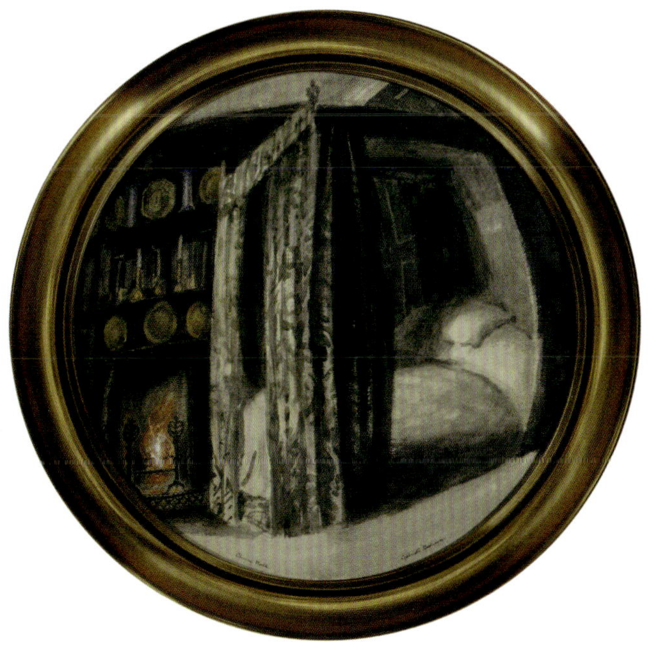

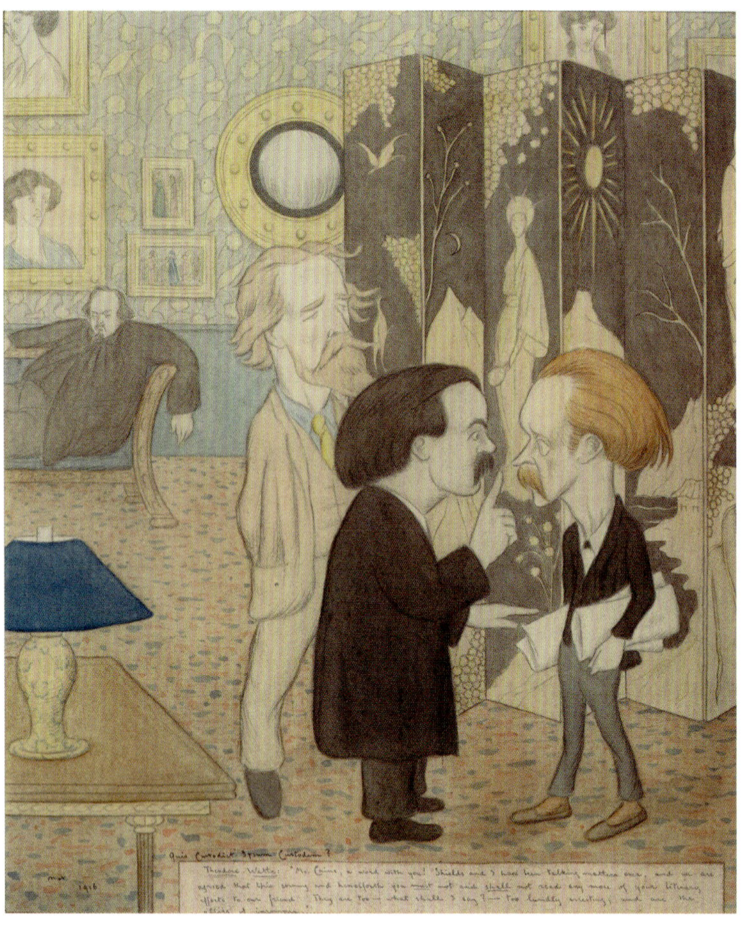

Holman Hunt also used the convex mirror as a way of exploring his own internal responses to the subject and removing it from the realism of the external world. His *Il Dolce far Niente* (which roughly translates as 'It is sweet to do nothing', cat. 28) was partly conceived as a riposte to his earlier *Awakening Conscience,* the religious overtones of the latter giving way to a sensuous appreciation of the sitter who is similarly presented at leisure in a domestic setting. Hunt started it in 1859 as a portrait of Annie Miller (the model for the *Awakening Conscience*), but subsequently replaced the original face with that of his fiancée and future wife, Fanny Waugh. In reworking the original version, he enlarged the canvas and added a convex mirror which, in contrast to the earlier picture, does not attempt to reflect the room in any coherent way: the reflection reveals a depth of space lacking in the 'real' space of the room with the figure lounging on the floor rather than seated as she faces us in the picture as if suggesting a different moment in time.[22] While Hunt was purportedly more concerned with material reality than Rossetti and his followers, his placement of the mirror and its illogical reflection suggest a shared concern to engage with his subject on a subjective, even fantastical level – a shift in emphasis that anticipates the inward-looking Symbolist art of the *fin de siècle*.

Fig. 13
Max Beerbohm (1872–1956)
'Quis Custodiet Ipsum Custodem', from 'Rossetti and his Friends', 1916
Graphite and watercolour on paper, 34.9 × 28.6 cm
Tate, London (A01058)

Cat. 28
William Holman Hunt (1827–1910)
Il Dolce far Niente, 1859–66, reworked 1874–5
Oil on canvas, 99.1 × 80 cm
Private Collection

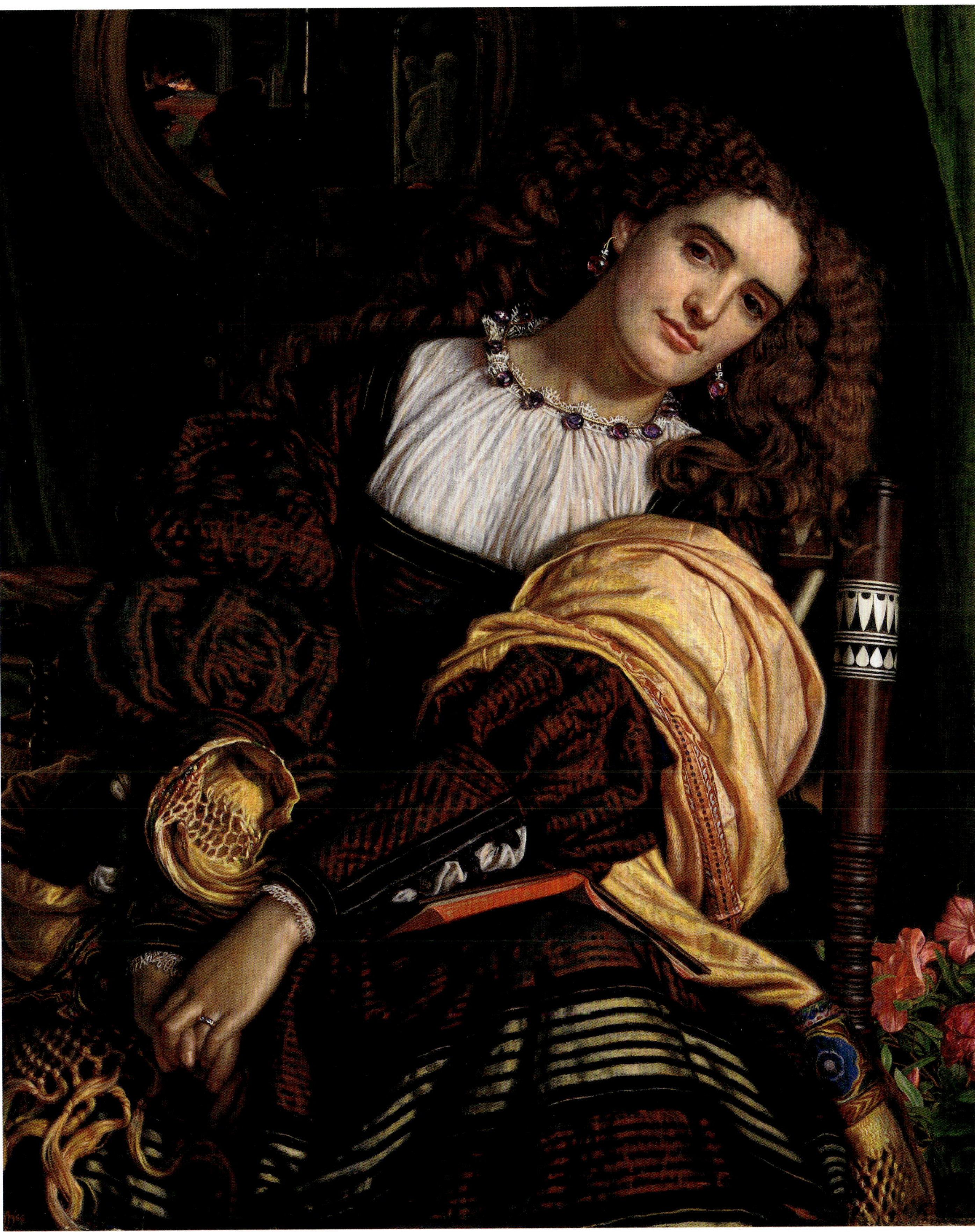

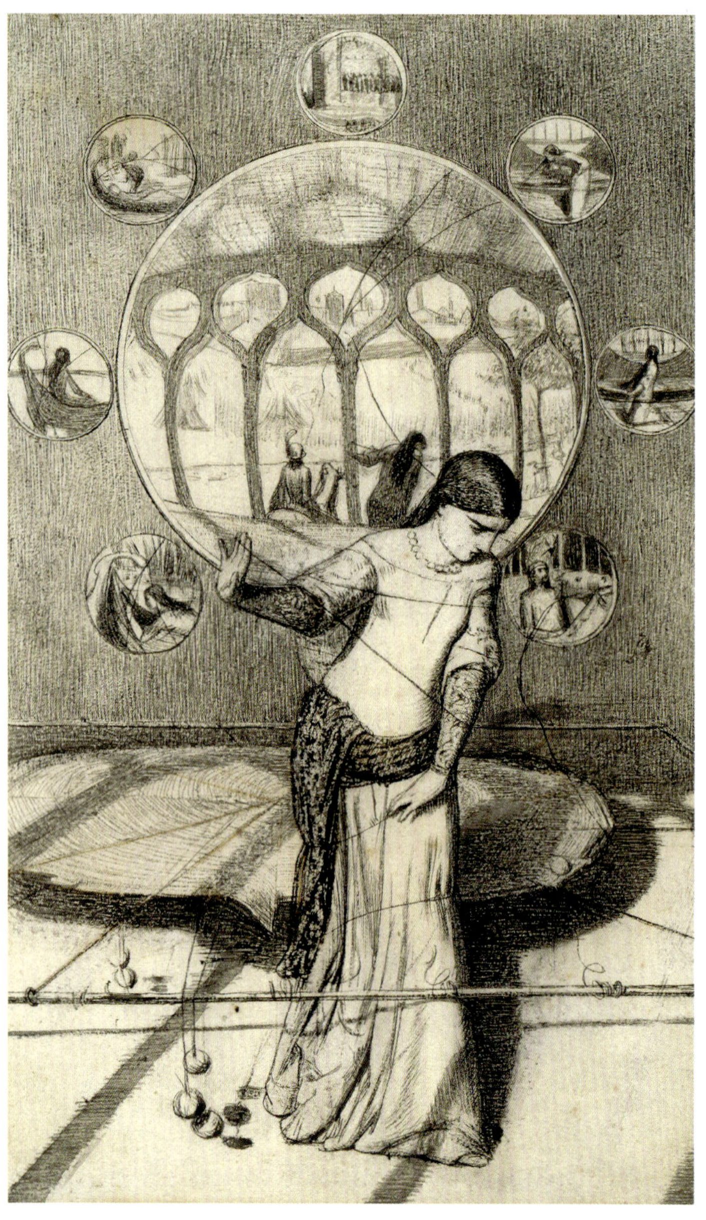

THE LADY OF SHALOTT

The ultimate form of artistic engagement with the *Arnolfini Portrait* can be found in the paintings that depict the Lady of Shalott. This subject encouraged a kind of magical realism through the pivotal role accorded the large, highly reflective mirror upon which the narrative turns. The subject itself derives from Tennyson's well-known poem, first published in 1832, which tells of an unidentified woman condemned by a curse not to engage with the outside world except for what she sees reflected in a magic mirror (see pp. 77–8 for the full poem). Obliged to reproduce on her loom the mirror's 'magic sights', she devotes herself to her task until the sight of Sir Lancelot riding out to Camelot leads her to defy the curse with tragic consequences that result in her death. Hunt was the first Pre-Raphaelite to depict the subject, in a drawing of 1850 (fig. 14) which reprises van Eyck's convex mirror in bringing the whole story together in a single image. The main scene is given over to the curse befalling the lady, with the roundels surrounding the mirror showing scenes that precede and follow the crisis, echoing the Passion cycle around the frame of van Eyck's mirror. By contrast, Elizabeth Eleanor Siddall's drawing of 1853 (cat. 29) places a large circular mirror to the far left of the composition in order to focus attention on the lady as she calmly looks away from it as if deciding her own fate. There is less emphasis here on the denouement that follows from the fatal look.

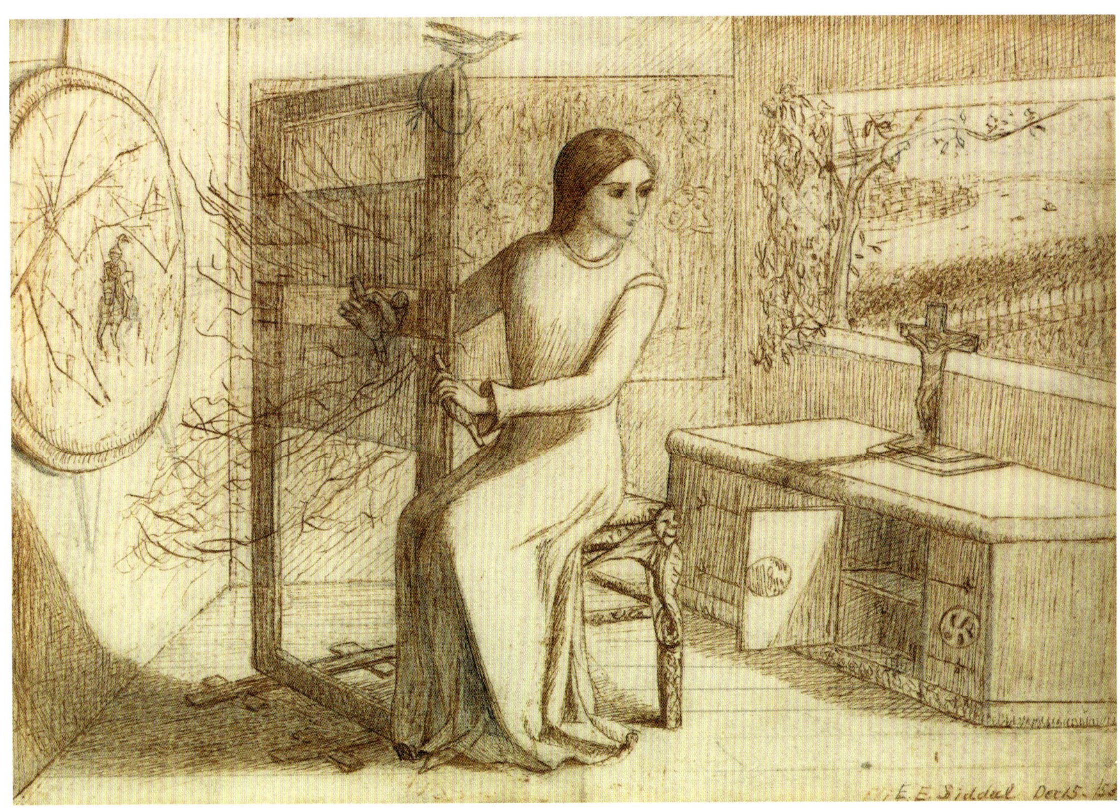

Fig. 14
William Holman Hunt (1827–1910)
The Lady of Shalott, 1850
Black chalk, pen and ink, 23.5 × 14.2 cm
National Gallery of Victoria, Melbourne
Felton Bequest, 1921 (1133-3)

Cat. 29
Elizabeth Eleanor Siddall (1829–1862)
The Lady of Shalott, 1853
Pen, ink and pencil on paper, 24.8 × 17.8 cm
The Maas Gallery

Hunt was to elaborate on his initial idea when, in 1857, he was commissioned to design an illustration of the scene for Edward Moxon's collection of Tennyson's poems (cat. 30) which resulted in the composition that was to preoccupy him, on and off, through to the completion in 1905 of the large oil now in the Wadsworth Atheneum, Hartford. The 1857 design is far more sinuous and elaborate than the earlier Hunt and Siddall drawings, with the sensuous curves of the woman with wild outflowing hair dominating the space, and the rebelliousness of her act underscored by the roundels depicting the Crucifixion and Christ in Majesty on either side. The later oil study which served as a template for the large version in Manchester (cat. 31) acknowledges this engraved design and also *Il Dolce far Niente* and the *Awakening Conscience* (see cats 28, 18), with the mirror reflecting the moment of revelation and the illuminated skeins of wool similarly functioning as a visual metaphor for the woman's distraught state of mind. These connections suggest a complex visual interplay between different kinds of subject, each stemming from Hunt's original encounter with the *Arnolfini Portrait.* The oil study was executed on panel in the minute, translucent original Pre-Raphaelite manner. It adapts many of the objects in the van Eyck picture, not just the mirror, but the wooden clogs in the foreground and the illuminated silver samovar topped

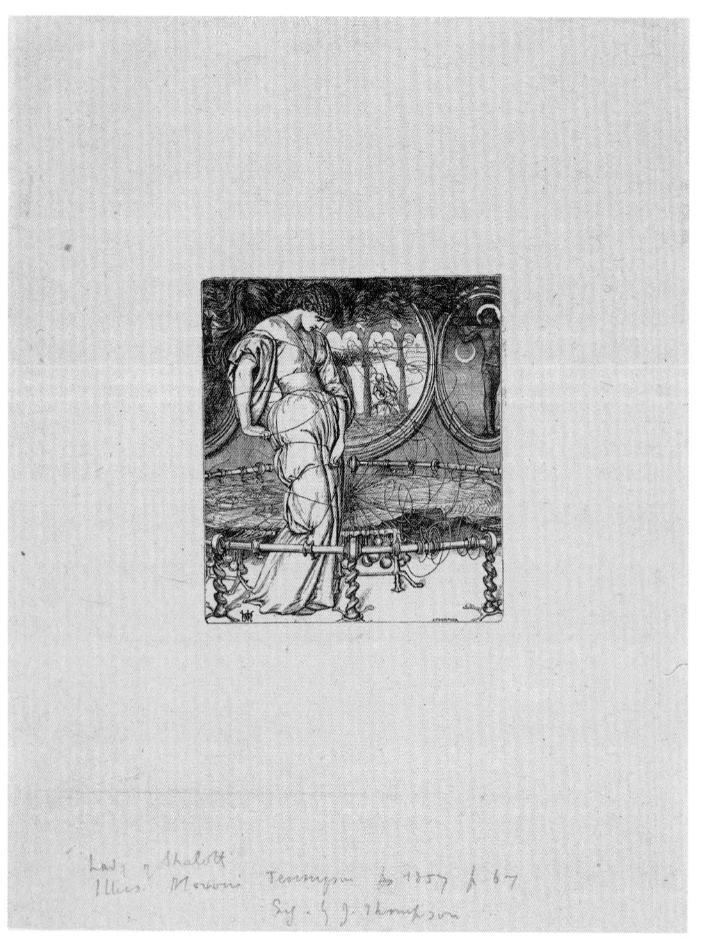

Cat. 30
William Holman Hunt (1827–1910)
The Lady of Shalott, engraved by J. Thompson, published 1857
Wood engraving on paper, 9.5 × 7.9 cm
Tate, London. Presented by Harold Hartley 1925 (N04052)

Cat. 31
William Holman Hunt (1827–1910)
The Lady of Shalott, about 1886–1905
Oil on wood, 44.4 × 34.1 cm
Manchester Art Gallery (1934.401)

with candles, a compound of the metalwork chandelier with the solitary lit candle in the *Arnolfini Portrait.* The lady herself is presented trapped between two painted images turned against the external world – the Agony in the Garden on the left, and Christ in Majesty on the right. Here the message of Christ's victory over temptation provides a visual counterpoint to the lady's surrender to it, making clear the moral import of the painting with the large extravagant mirror disclosing a deeper truth than what the artist termed mere 'bald realism'.[23] Indeed for Hunt the lady was more than a fictitious character – she was the embodiment of the artist who, entrusted with a mission, fails to deliver it by succumbing to personal desires. Hunt believed himself at the end of his career to be the only member of the original Brotherhood to have abided consistently by its founding principles, and his painting looks back to the *Arnolfini Portrait,* acknowledging other responses to it along the way, while anticipating what Elizabeth Prettejohn has termed the more problematic worlds of the future – the realms of Freudian psychoanalysis, Surrealism and Science Fiction.[24]

Hunt's successive re-workings of the *Lady of Shalott* established the approach for other interpretations of the poem which employ similar large circular mirrors to underscore the narcissistic, obsessive overtones of the subject. These objects appear in the pictures of younger artists who had the opportunity to view early Pre-Raphaelite works at the retrospective exhibitions held in honour of Rossetti, Millais and Hunt in the 1880s.[25] While John William Waterhouse's painting of 1894 (cat. 32) reaches out in a new direction with its broad painterly execution and lack of symbolic detail, it is totally indebted in other ways to the Pre-Raphaelite prototype. Waterhouse evidently tried hard not to imitate Hunt, but the iconographic scheme established by the older artist had become so integral to the subject that he could not avoid it altogether. The mirror and its reflections thus hark back to Hunt's design, while the small devotional

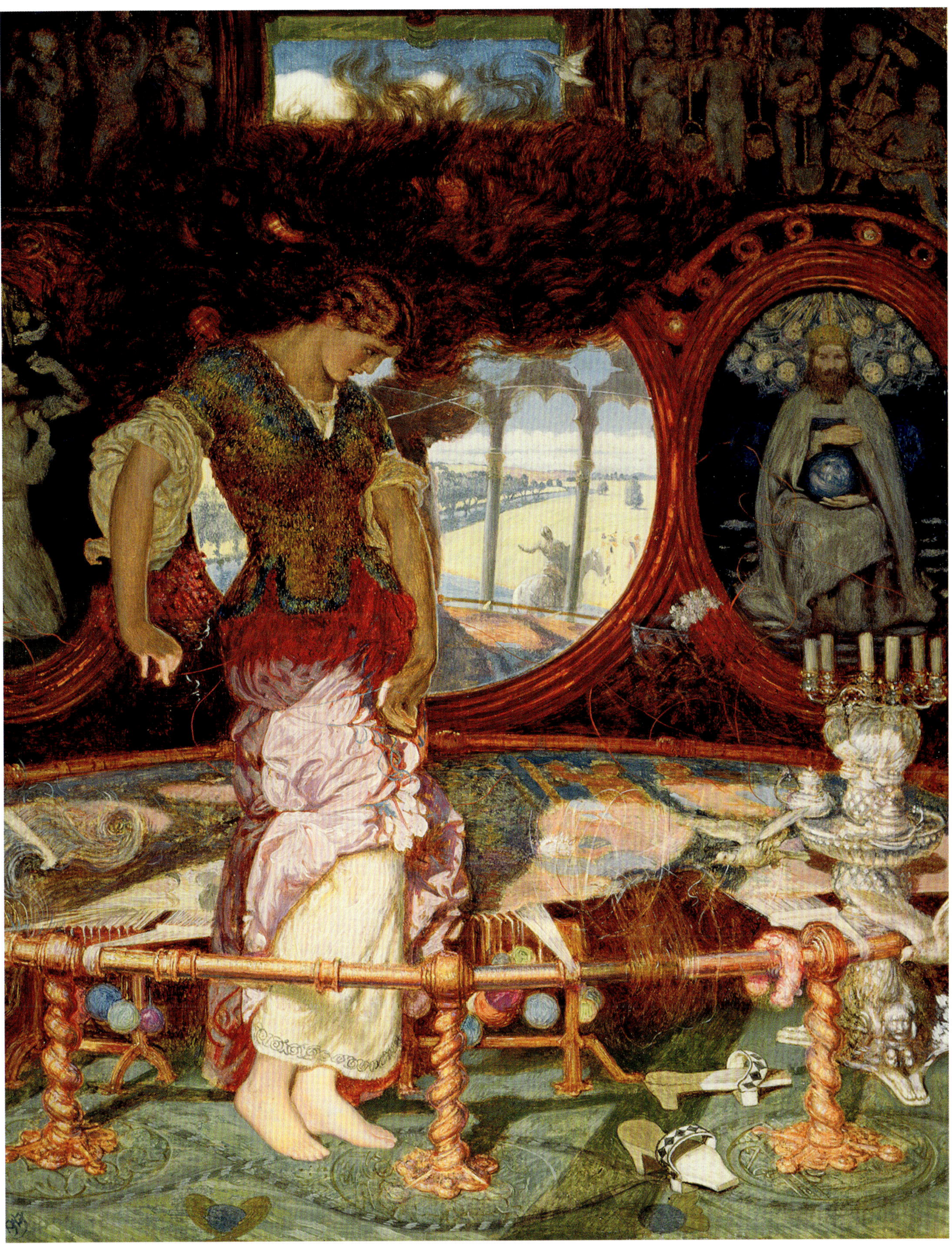

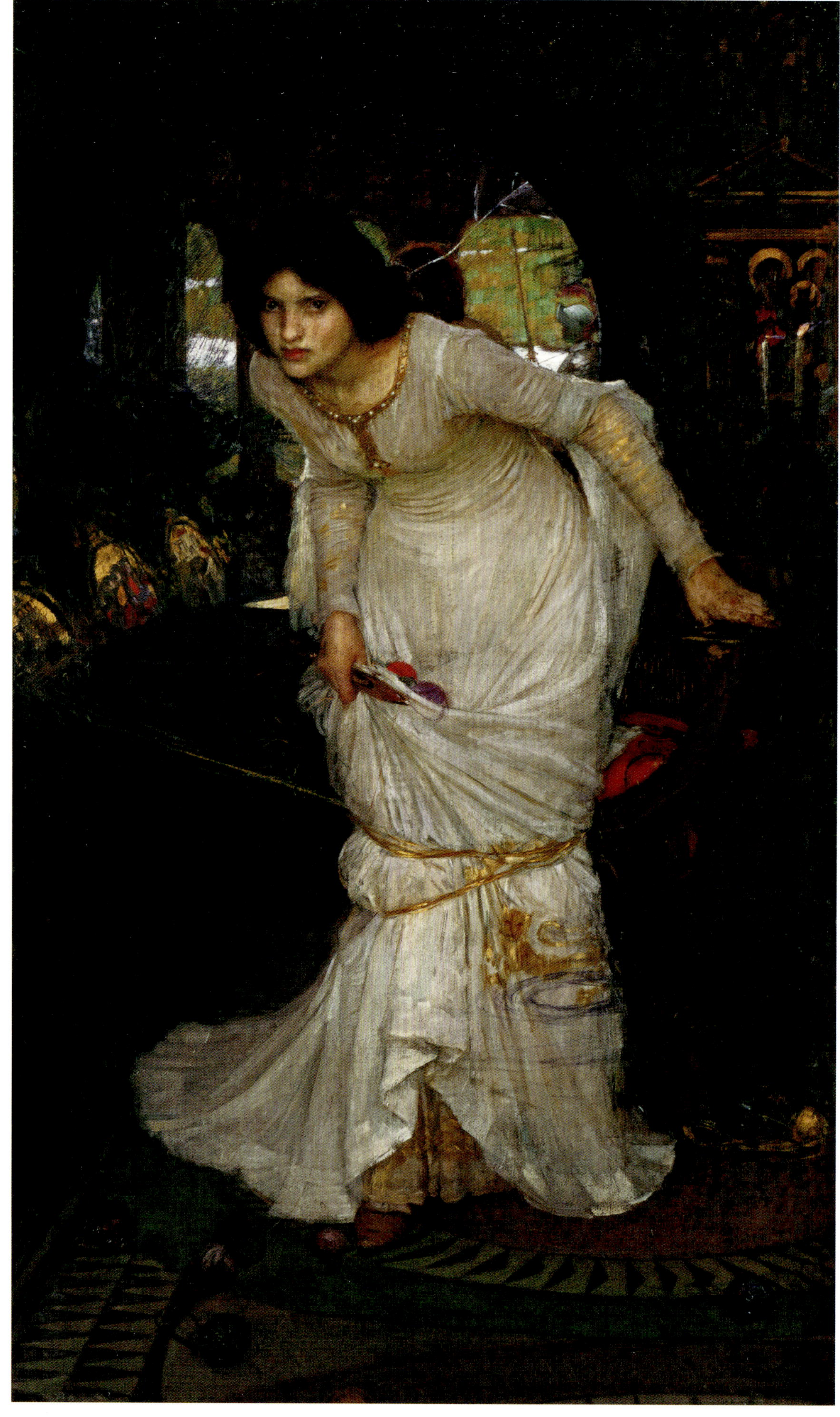

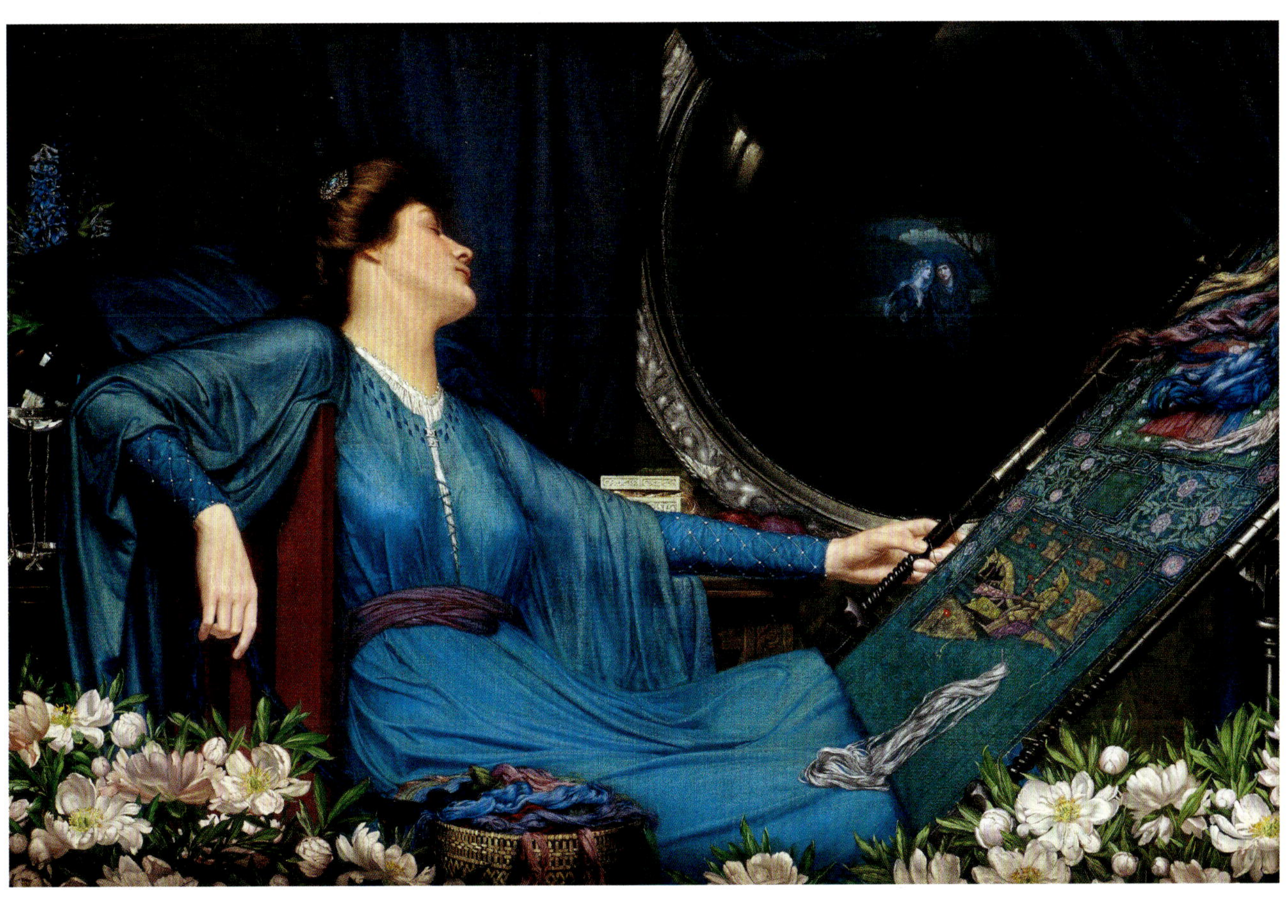

Cat. 32

John William Waterhouse (1849–1917)

The Lady of Shalott, 1894

Oil on canvas, 142.2 × 86.3 cm

Leeds Museums and Galleries (Leeds Art Gallery, LEEAG.1895.0004)

Cat. 33

Sidney Meteyard (1868–1947)

'I am Half-Sick of Shadows, Said the Lady of Shalott', 1913

Oil on canvas, 76 × 114.5 cm

Private Collection, courtesy of Martin Beisly

Cat. 34
Edward Burne-Jones (1833–1898)
Margaret Burne-Jones, 1885–6
Oil on canvas, 91.2 × 66 cm
Private Collection

altar is reminiscent of Millais's *Mariana*, which Waterhouse would have seen at the retrospective of the artist's work at the Grosvenor Gallery in 1886. By contrast, Sidney Meteyard's *'I am Half-Sick of Shadows, Said the Lady of Shalott'* (cat. 33) revives the early minute Pre-Raphaelite mode of execution to illustrate the moment that precedes Lancelot's intrusion into the poem, when the lady, wearied at the sight of 'two young lovers lately wed' cast by the magic mirror, closes her eyes to its tantalising shadowy reflections.

'A DREAM WITHIN A DREAM'

It has been suggested that the convex mirror and dark blue tonality of Meteyard's picture were influenced by Burne-Jones's portrait of his daughter Margaret (cat. 34), which hung in the hall of The Grange, greeting visitors with its haunting presence. Burne-Jones, who judged the *Arnolfini Portrait* to be 'the finest picture in the world', admired it especially for what he termed its 'extreme darkness'.[26] A similar quality can be found in the portrait of Margaret, whose bedroom is revealed in what a critic described as 'a mirror worthy of Van Eyck'.[27] Here the mirror functions as a kind of halo (as in cat. 19) exaggerating the real and reflected form of her head and mirror-like eyes as if to emphasise the detached interiorised quality the artist so prized in his youngest child. Painted a few years prior to Margaret's marriage to the classicist John William Mackail, the portrait conveys something of the extreme attachment and possessiveness Burne-Jones felt for his daughter, the Marian connotations of the blue dress reinforcing the idea of remoteness and perfection.

The hypnotic power of Burne-Jones's portrait lies in the contrast it establishes between the idealised presence of Margaret's body and the distorted reflection in the mirror, the latter reminiscent of the looming furniture in Treffry Dunn's rifle-sight view into Rossetti's bedroom. By the time it was painted the practice of presenting a figure with its back to a convex mirror had become something of a trope in Pre-Raphaelite and Aesthetic painting, the mirror functioning to confuse the spectator's perception of space while preserving the integrity of the depicted subject at its centre. The viewer rarely, if ever, is offered the distorted anamorphic reflection of a face in a convex mirror that so horrified Mrs Haweis (see p. 44).

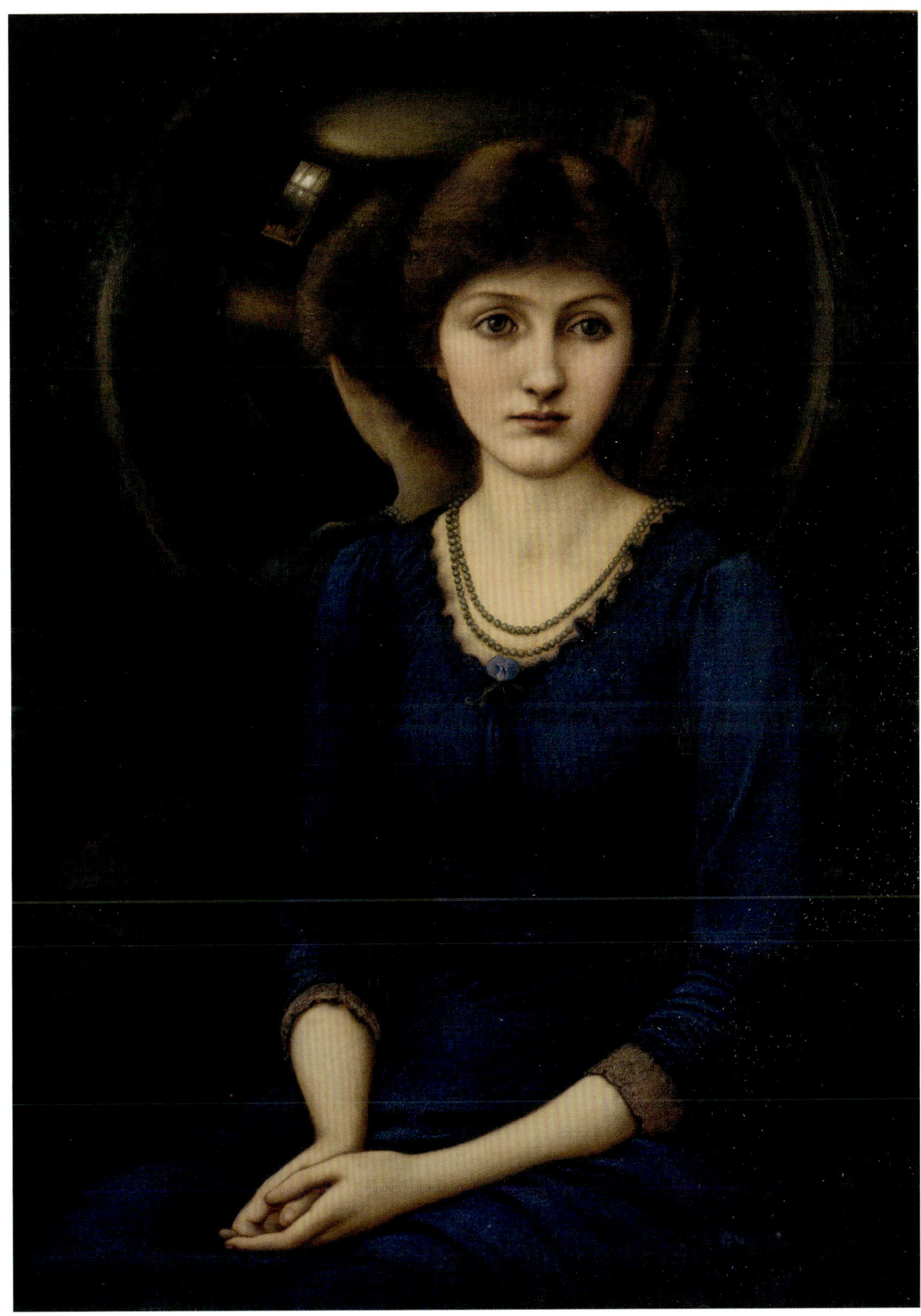

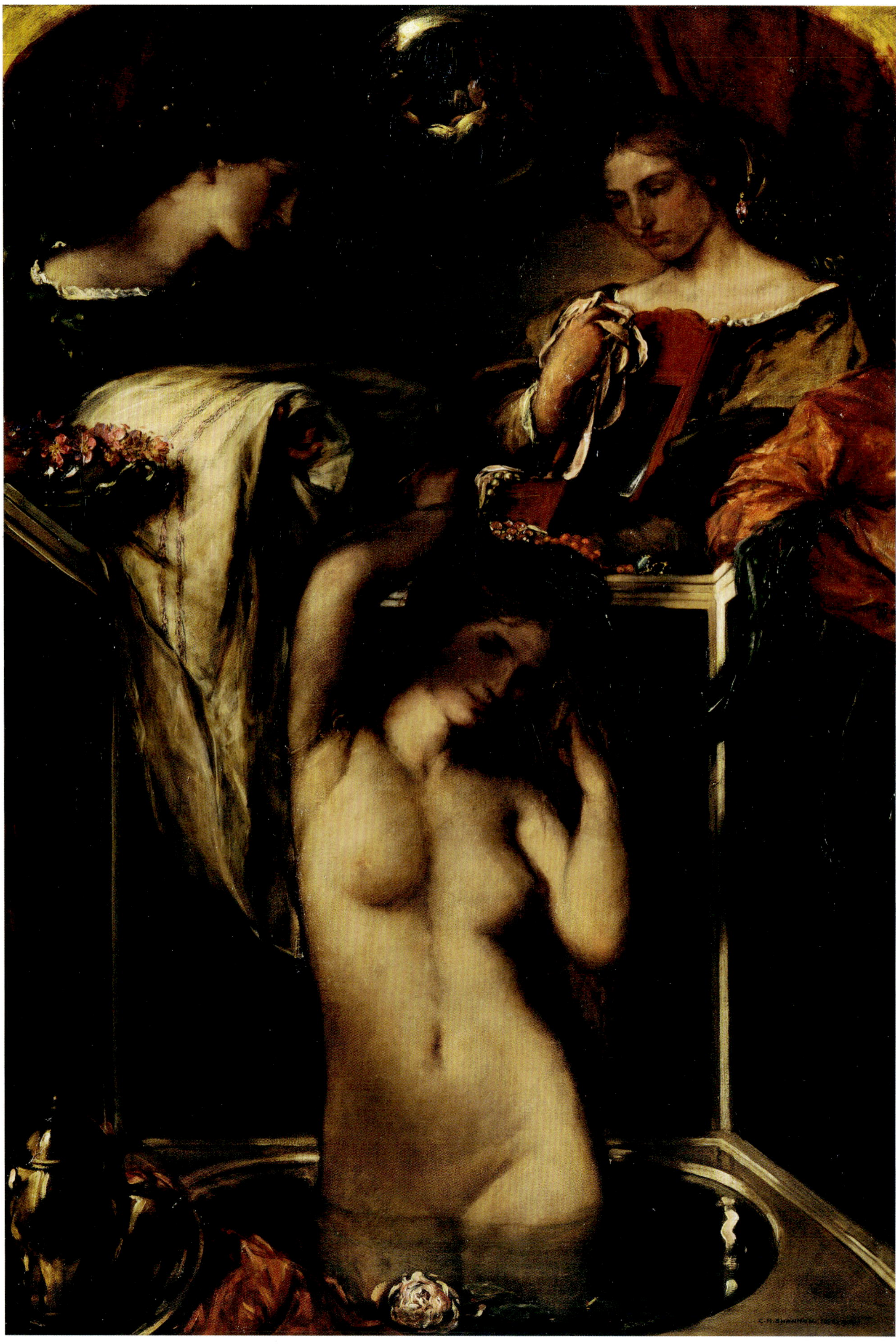

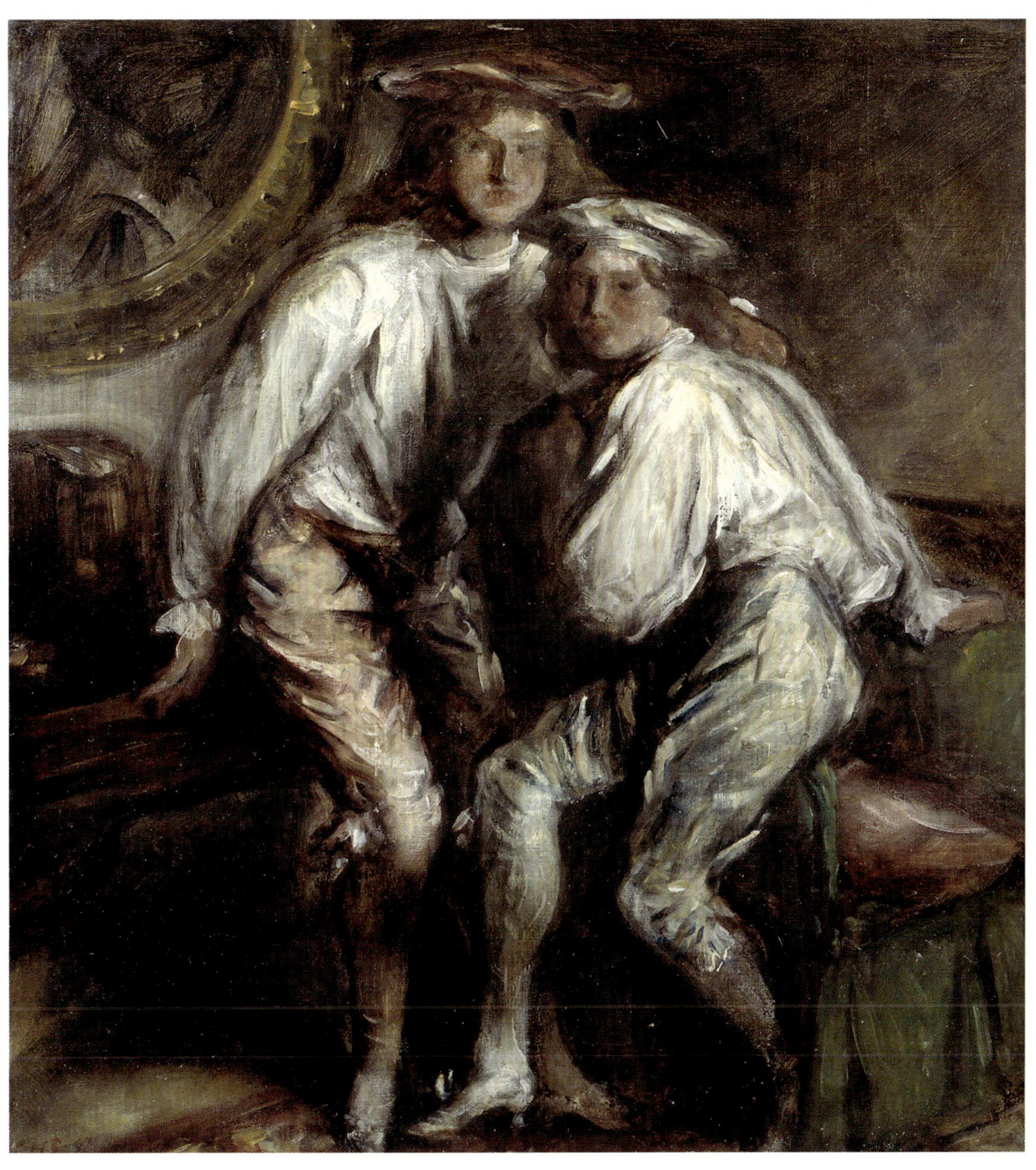

Cat. 35

Charles Shannon (1863–1937)

The Bath of Venus, 1898–1904

Oil on canvas, 146 × 97.8 cm

Tate, London. Presented by Francis Howard 1940 (N05160)

Cat. 36

Charles Shannon (1863–1937)

Les Marmitons, 1897

Oil on canvas on board, 39 × 36.6 cm

Tate, London. Purchased 1942 (N05363)

As a device that provided an ambiguous link with the external world, the convex mirror brought van Eyck, via the Pre-Raphaelites, into the imaginings of a younger generation of Symbolist painters who utilised it to de-materialise form in capturing a moment of fleeting penumbral beauty. Among them were the long-time partners in life and art, Charles Shannon and Charles Ricketts (the latter was to present Rossetti's *Lucrezia Borgia* to the Tate in 1916, cat. 24). Rossetti's influence, combined with other sources ranging from classical antiquity to the ideal nudes of Titian, can be found in Shannon's work in which mirrors were frequently employed to both suggest and underplay ideas of doubling and reflection. In the *Bath of Venus* (cat. 35), the play of light across a variety of shadowy reflective surfaces heightens the sensuality of the theme, with the dark enclosed forms of the pool and mirror acting as metaphors for containment and contemplative looking. In another work, *Les Marmitons* (cat. 36), the transitory impression of two women caught posing as male scullions is accentuated by the hazy surface of what appears to be a large circular mirror positioned behind them on the wall.

VELÁZQUEZ, VAN EYCK AND THE MODERN DOMESTIC PORTRAIT

The *Arnolfini Portrait* had a further phase of influence filtered through Velázquez's best-known work. In the seventeenth century, when the painting belonged to the Spanish Royal Collection, it was seen by Velázquez and perhaps prompted his *Las Meninas*, which featured what was to become the most famous mirror next to the *Arnolfini Portrait* in the history of Western art (fig. 15). In contrast to the sharp reflections of van Eyck's mirror, the dark rectangular mirror in Velázquez's group portrait conjures up the ghostly presence of the King and Queen of Spain who do not appear elsewhere in the composition. This has given rise to conflicting interpretations about how to read the painting, with some suggesting that the mirror might actually be a painted portrait, and others, perhaps more convincingly, arguing that it represents the mirrored image of what the artist is shown painting on canvas, with the whole picture therefore intended to be read as if painted from the royal couple's perspective.

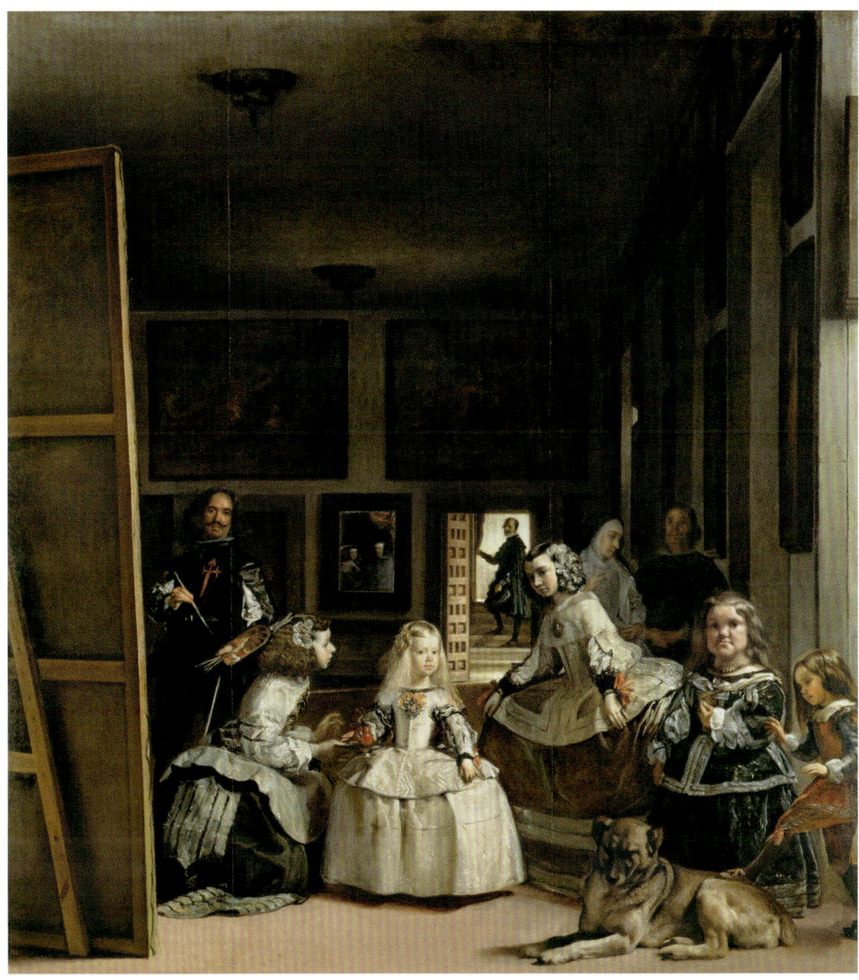

Fig. 15
Diego Velázquez (1599–1660)
'Las Meninas' or the Family of Philip IV, about 1656
Oil on canvas, 318 cm × 276 cm
Museo Nacional del Prado, Madrid (P01174)

Whatever experience the original Pre-Raphaelites had of *Las Meninas* would have been through John Phillip, a Scottish painter immersed in Spanish culture who visited Spain three times between 1851 and 1860. Following his final trip, Phillip completed his partial copy of *Las Meninas* (cat. 37) moving the mirror to the very centre of the composition, the position it occupied in most Victorian mirror paintings. From 1868 this copy hung in the Diploma Gallery at the Royal Academy where it was seen by many artists. A dark tonality and broad execution characterises many later nineteenth-century re-imaginings of van Eyck, as painters ranged beyond the Pre-Raphaelite principle of minuteness to embrace the work of more painterly Old Masters such as Velázquez, Titian and Parmigianino, all of whom employed mirrors in their works for purposes of illusionism and deformation. Velázquez's 'impressionist' manner was unlike the hard-edged style of van Eyck, but certain artists, such as Millais, saw the Spaniard's work as an extension of the scientific method and psychological realism widely admired in the earlier artist.[28] The perceptual ambiguities of Velázquez's work,

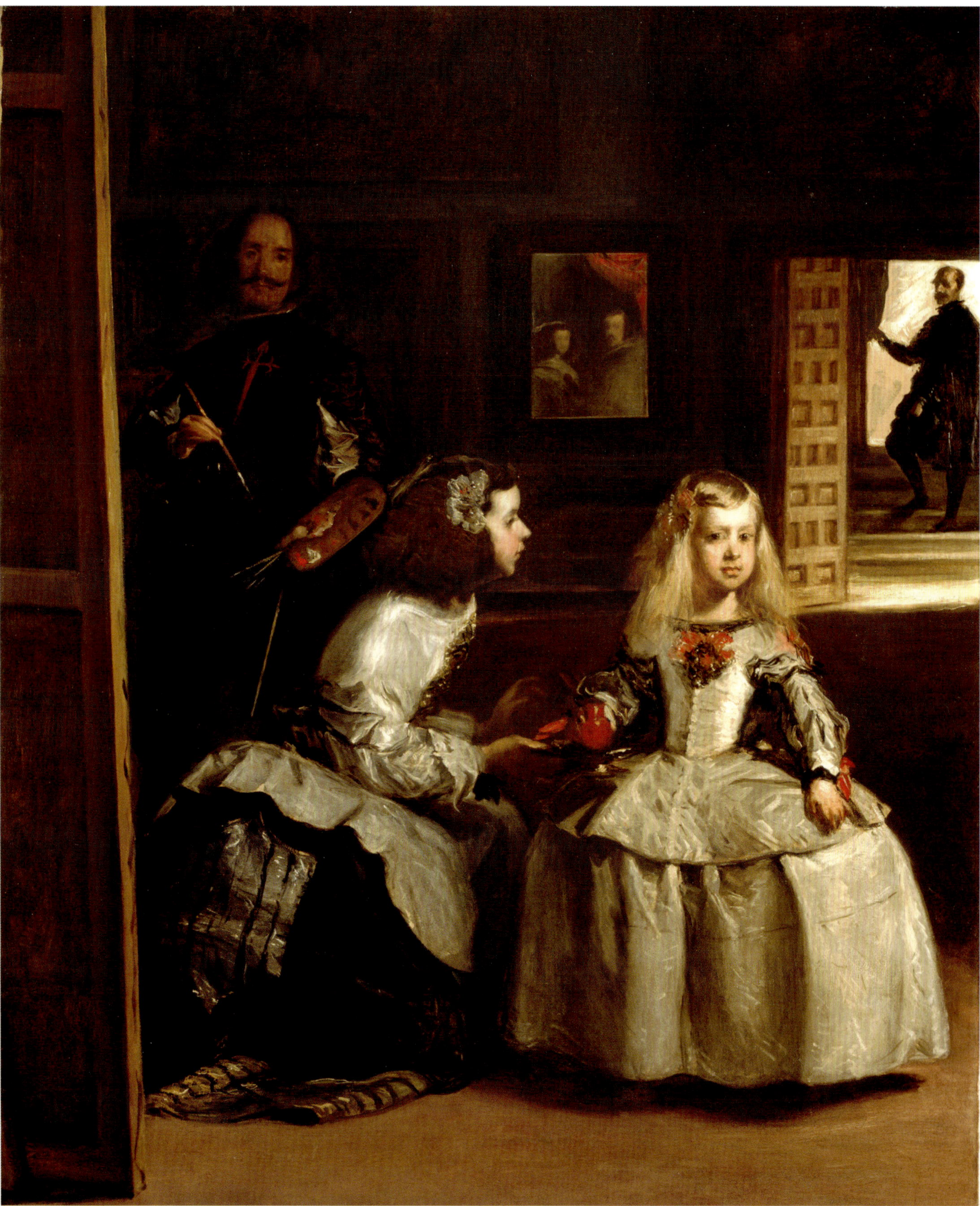

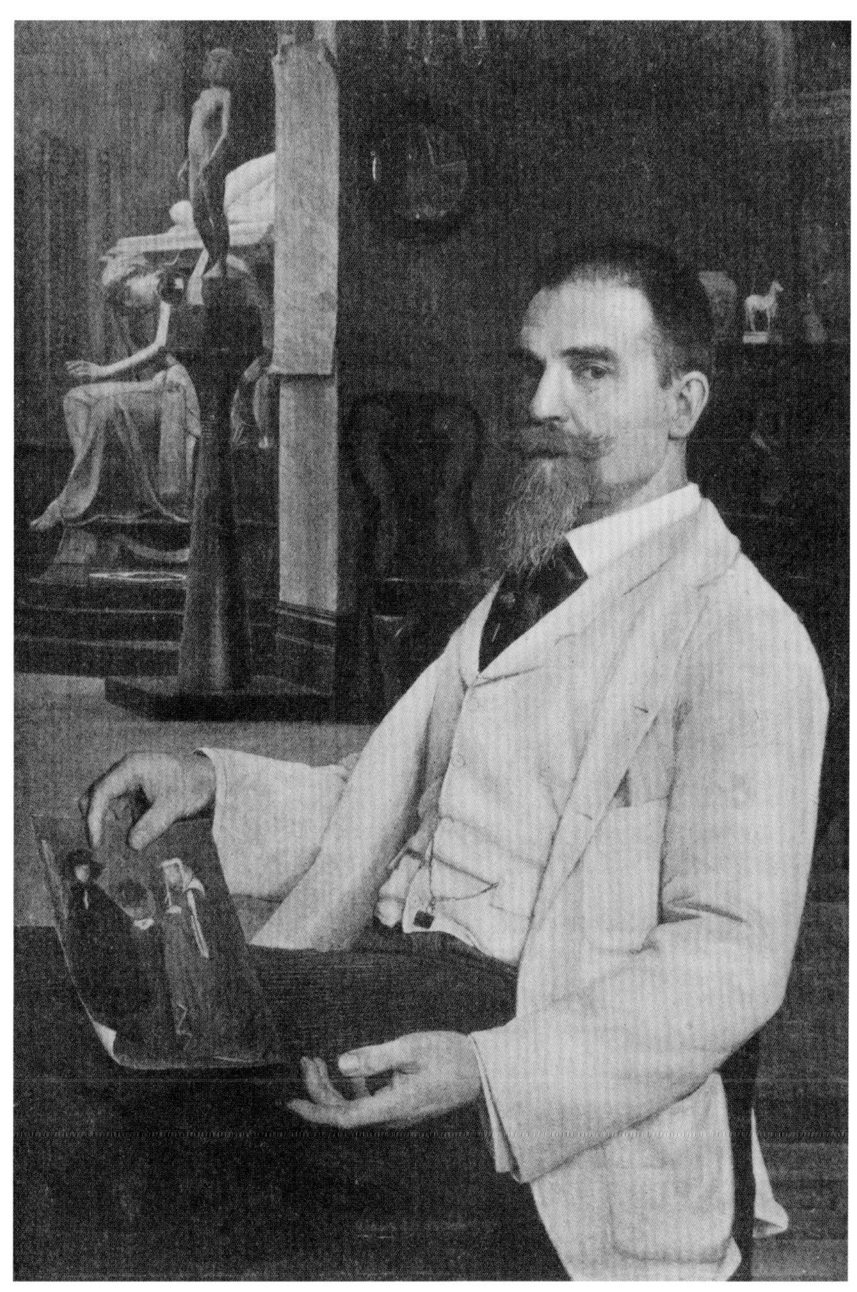

Cat. 37
John Phillip, RA (1817–1867)
Partial copy of 'Las Meninas', 1862.
Oil on canvas, 185 × 148 cm
Royal Academy of Arts, London (03/1097)

Cat. 38
Wolfram Onslow Ford (1879–1956)
My Father, reproduction of the missing original printed in *The Studio,* vol. 25, 1902
Tate Archives, London (35885–1001)

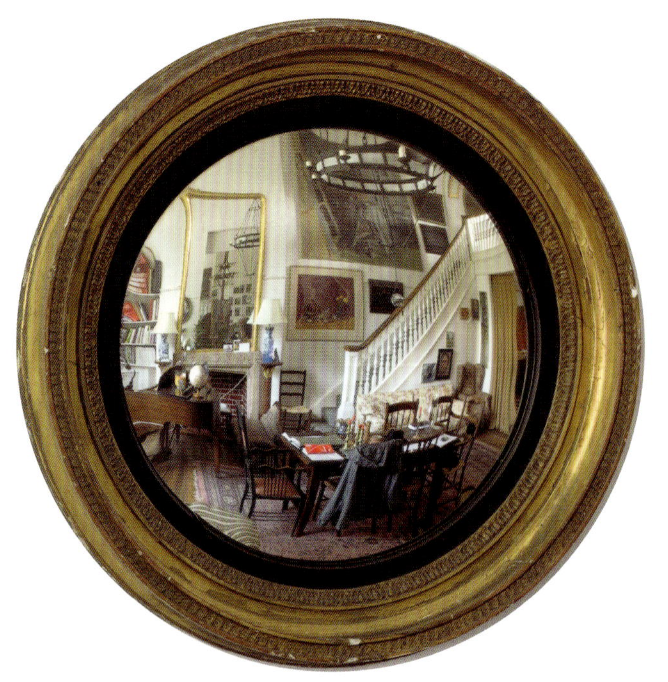

Cat. 39

Convex mirror used by William Orpen (1878–1931)

63 diameter × 8 cm

Private Ownership

Cat. 40

William Orpen (1878–1931)

The Mirror, 1900

Oil on canvas, 50.8 × 40.6 cm

Tate, London. Presented by Mrs Coutts Michie through the Art Fund in memory of the George McCulloch Collection 1913 (N02940)

combined with the *Arnolfini Portrait's* iconic status among artists, encouraged a further new proliferation of domestic subjects featuring modern-day round and convex mirrors. Generally devoid of literary or mythological content, and neither medievalising nor self-consciously historicist, these were by and large set in the present, proclaiming artistic virtuosity and the authority of the artist's gaze. There emerged a distinct category of self-portraiture as painters self-consciously referenced van Eyck or Velázquez to fashion and probe their own artistic identities. Wolfram Onslow Ford's portrait *My Father* (cat. 38) which presents the sculptor Edward Onslow Ford in his studio, is unique among this type in being an overtly Pre-Raphaelite work in which the faithful reproduction of the *Arnolfini Portrait* held up by the sculptor acts as a manifesto for the principle of mimesis and craftsmanship that linked the two artists across time, the convex mirror on the wall reinforcing the idea of homage.

Of all the artists who knowingly acknowledged van Eyck and other past masters in portraiture around the turn of the last century, William Orpen stands out for his persistent use of mirrors to capture his own self-image at a distance (cat. 39). The painter's obsession with his reflected image has been linked to his own deep-felt insecurity, which apparently stemmed from his overhearing as a child his parents bemoaning his appearance: the distorting and diminishing effects provided by the convex surface of mirrors in his work relate to the 'otherness of self' that became a hallmark of his art. An early example is *The Mirror* (cat. 40), dominated by a circular mirror that reflects on a minuscule scale the artist at work on his easel in his lodgings with a woman by his side. In deference to van Eyck, the reflection includes a modern-day chandelier and lamp in place of the brass candelabra with burning candle in the original. Seated in the foreground, but not reflected in the mirror, is another woman, the model and artist's then fiancée, Emily Scoble, who is presented as if gazing back at the painter. As with the *Arnolfini Portrait* and *Las Meninas*, the mirror captures a particular private moment, but through it an iconographic type so instantly recognisable that John Rothenstein, director of the Tate from 1938 to 1964, could only regard it as little more than an essay in assimilation rather than an engagement with the past that was as original in its way as the art of the Pre-Raphaelites.[29]

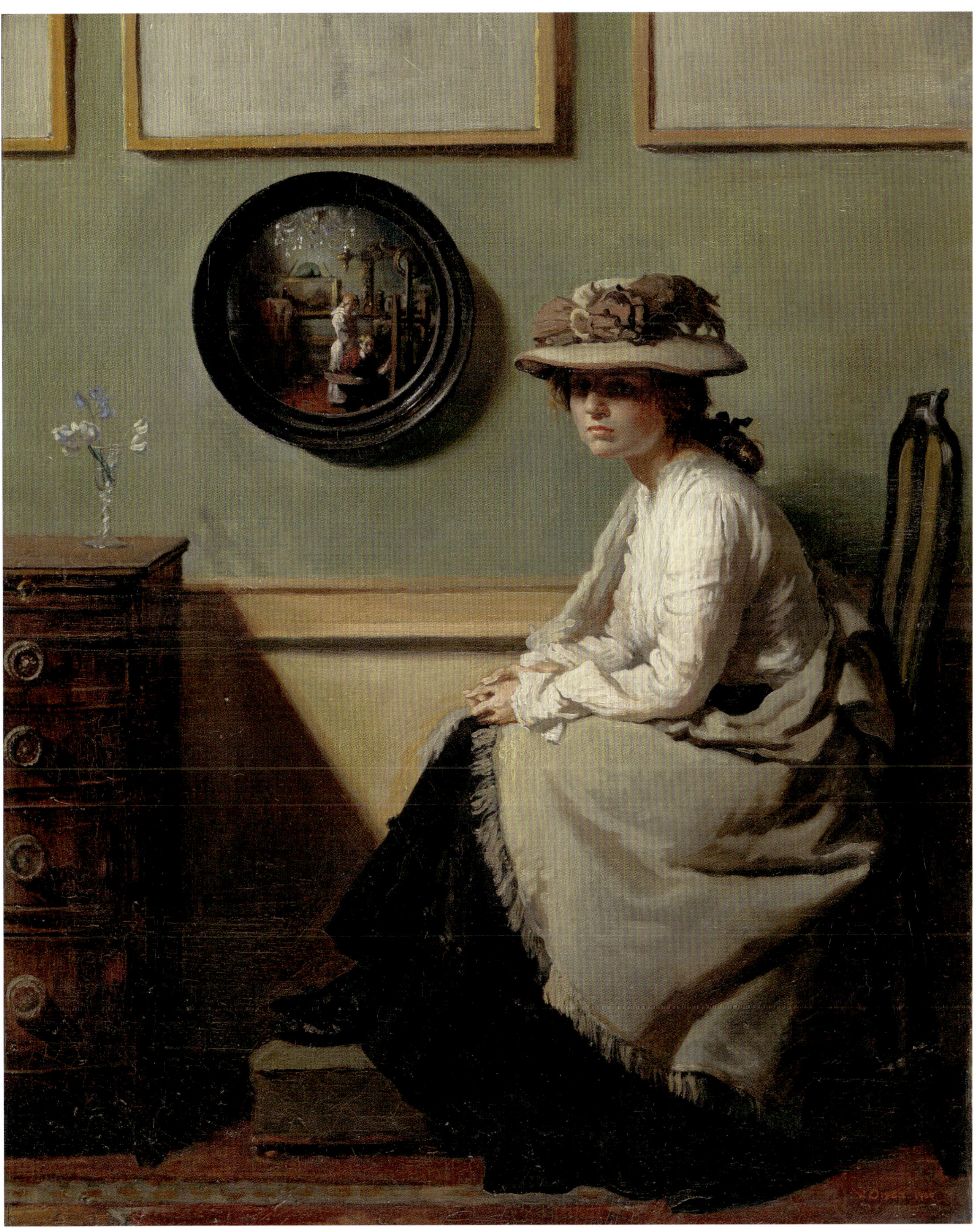

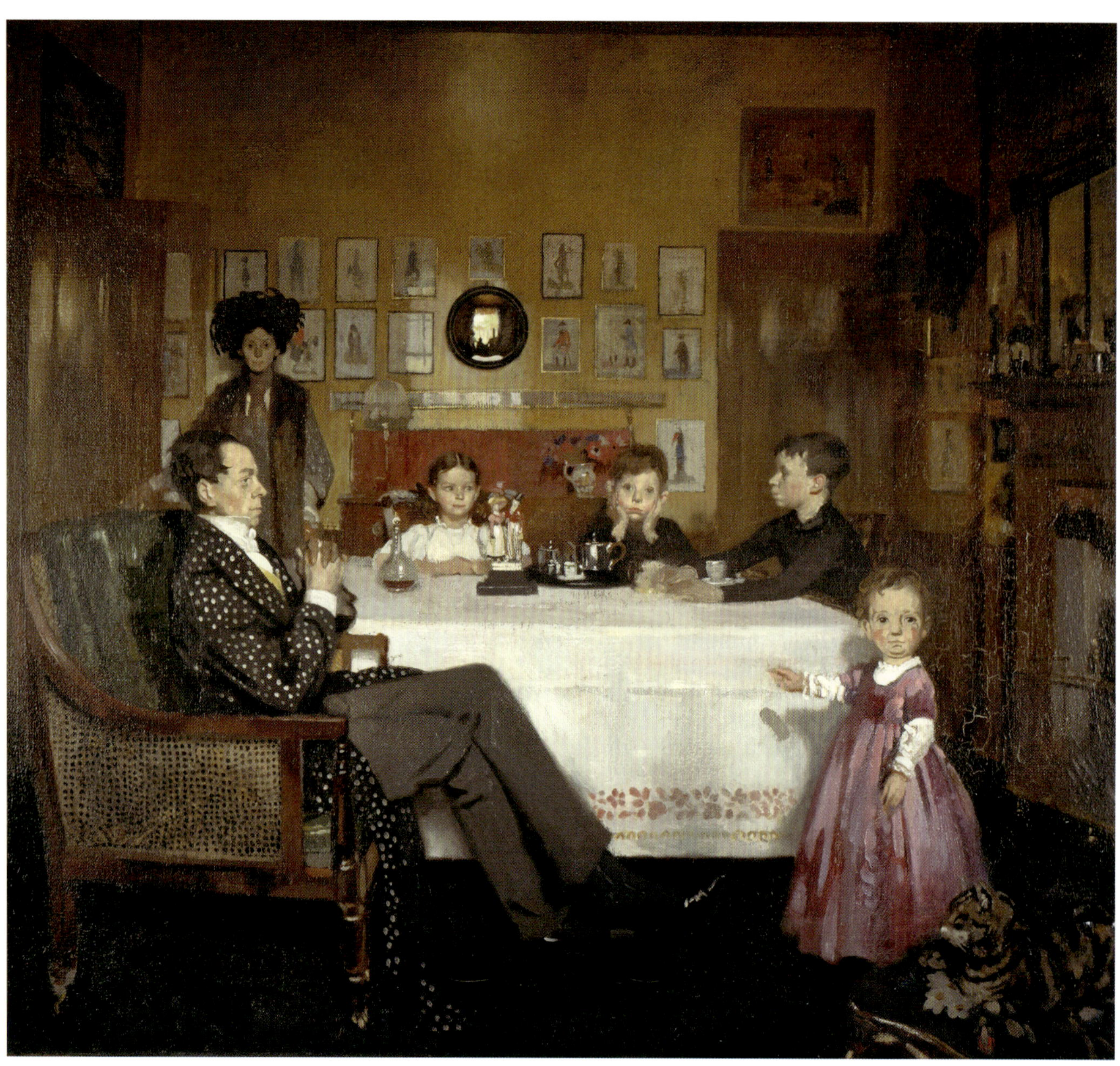

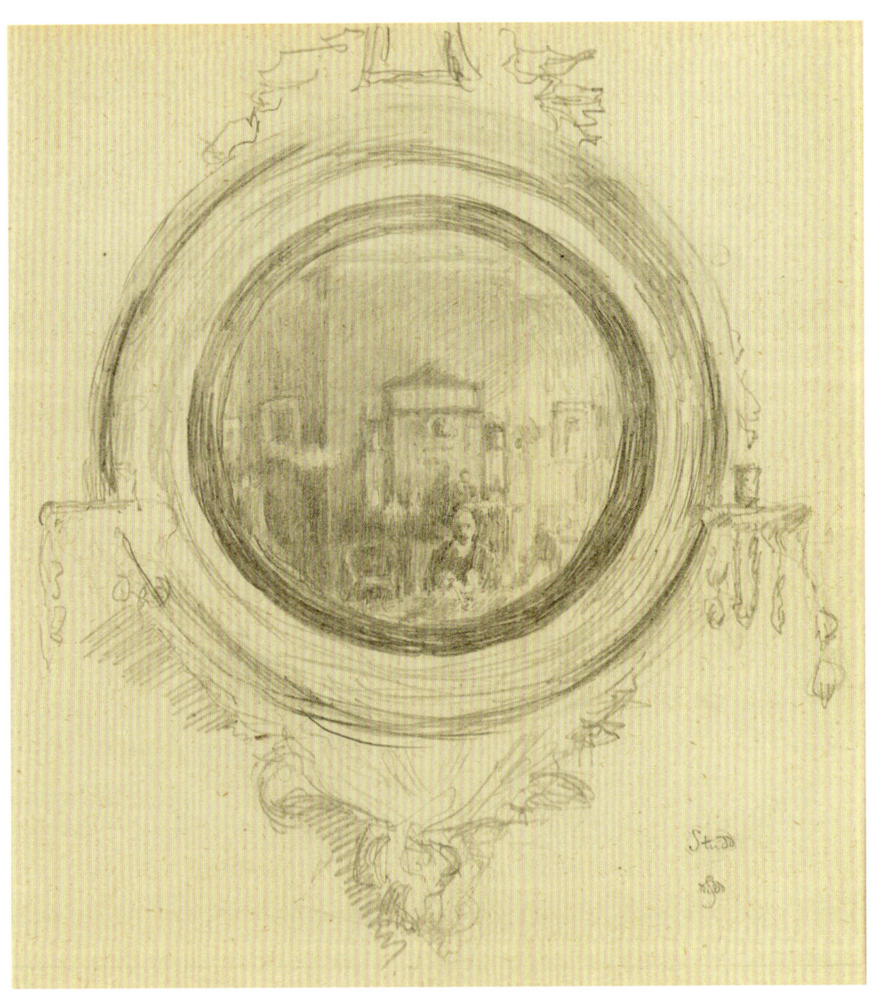

Cat. 41
William Orpen (1878–1931)
A Bloomsbury Family, 1907
Oil on canvas, 86.5 × 91.5 cm
Scottish National Gallery of Modern Art, Edinburgh (GMA 881)

Cat. 42
Arthur Studd (1863–1919)
Self Portrait in a Round Mirror, early twentieth century
Pencil on paper, 13 × 11.5 cm
Private Collection

A similar mirror appears in Orpen's *A Bloomsbury Family* (cat. 41), which also looks back to the past in presenting its modern-day subject. This painting depicts the Nicholson family (the painters William Nicholson and Mabel Pryde, and their children) formally posed around a table in the dining room of their house in Mecklenburgh Square, Bloomsbury. Just discernible in the reflection of the mirror placed in the centre of the wall is a silhouette of the artist at his easel with a model – in acknowledgement of *The Mirror*, and through it Velázquez, van Eyck and the Pre-Raphaelites. As with these precedents, the painting offers a heightened perception of its subject as if the artist were attempting to capture the scene from both his own and each sitter's perspective. Here, the discreet way in which Orpen has staged himself at work on his modern-day conversation piece mirrors the stultifying formality of the occasion, itself subtly undermined by the children's expressions of boredom and amusement.

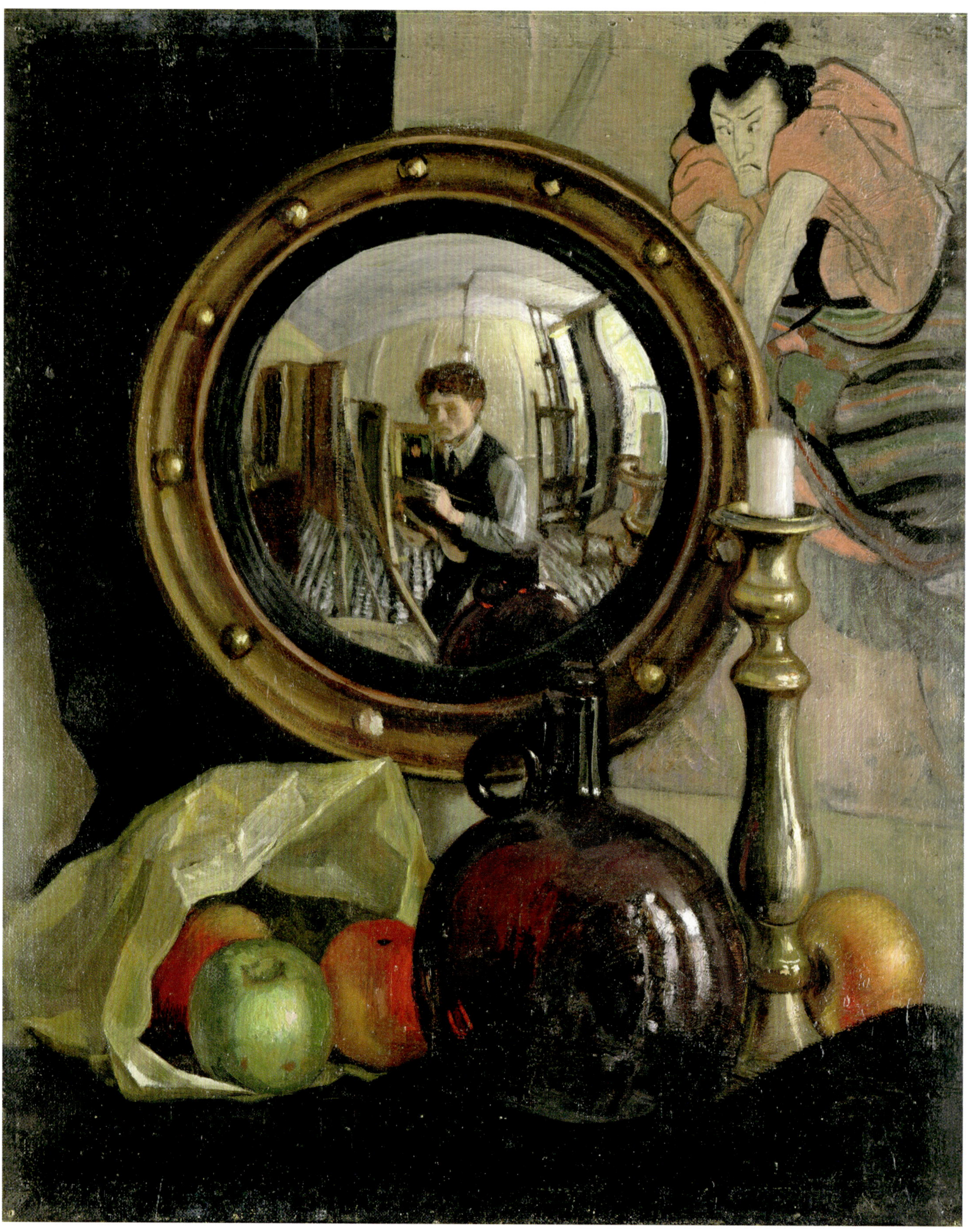

Cat. 43
Mark Gertler (1891–1939)
Still Life with Self Portrait, 1918
Oil on canvas, 50.8 × 40.6 cm
Leeds Museums and Galleries (Leeds Art Gallery, LEEAG. 1956.0001.0003)

Convex and circular mirrors became familiar motifs in British portraiture of the early twentieth century, often used to admit light into a room through painted reflections of apertures and thresholds into unseen spaces. Their inclusion allowed artists to depict reflections that conveyed notions about themselves, thereby destabilising as well as asserting identity. By focusing exclusively on the actual reflected image, independent of its surrounds, Arthur Studd's ghostly reflected form in cat. 42 can just be picked out amidst a complex ensemble of shapes and tones, the recognition of which is largely dependent on successive re-interpretations of van Eyck. By contrast, Mark Gertler's reflection in *Still Life with Self Portrait* (cat. 43) comprises part of a still-life subject in which the artist is shown painting in a mirror with the studio reflected again in the surface of a bottle that forms part of the inanimate group he is copying. In this seemingly everyday scene, the real and reflected parts of the image draw on earlier iconographic and representational models to both question and affirm existence. Thus the Samurai in the print partly obscured by the mirror, poised as if about to strike the reflected subject, evokes the *memento mori* theme traditionally associated with still life, while the allusion to what is believed to be van Eyck's self-image preserved in the reflection of his mirror in the *Arnolfini Portrait* upholds the idea of seizing a human presence through the very act of painting.

It was largely through self-portraiture and everyday genre subjects that the *Arnolfini Portrait* lived on in the artistic imagination. In 1924, the centenary of the National Gallery's foundation, it was ranked one of the most popular works in the entire collection and a favourite among painters. By this time the portrait's seemingly neutral realism was seen as embodying an enduring compositional innovation, providing a link between the Pre-Raphaelite generation and the more matter-of-fact approaches to realism that predominated around the turn of the century. In its high precision and the mysterious reflections of its mirror, the *Arnolfini Portrait* could be said to have literally 'shaped' a tradition in British art.

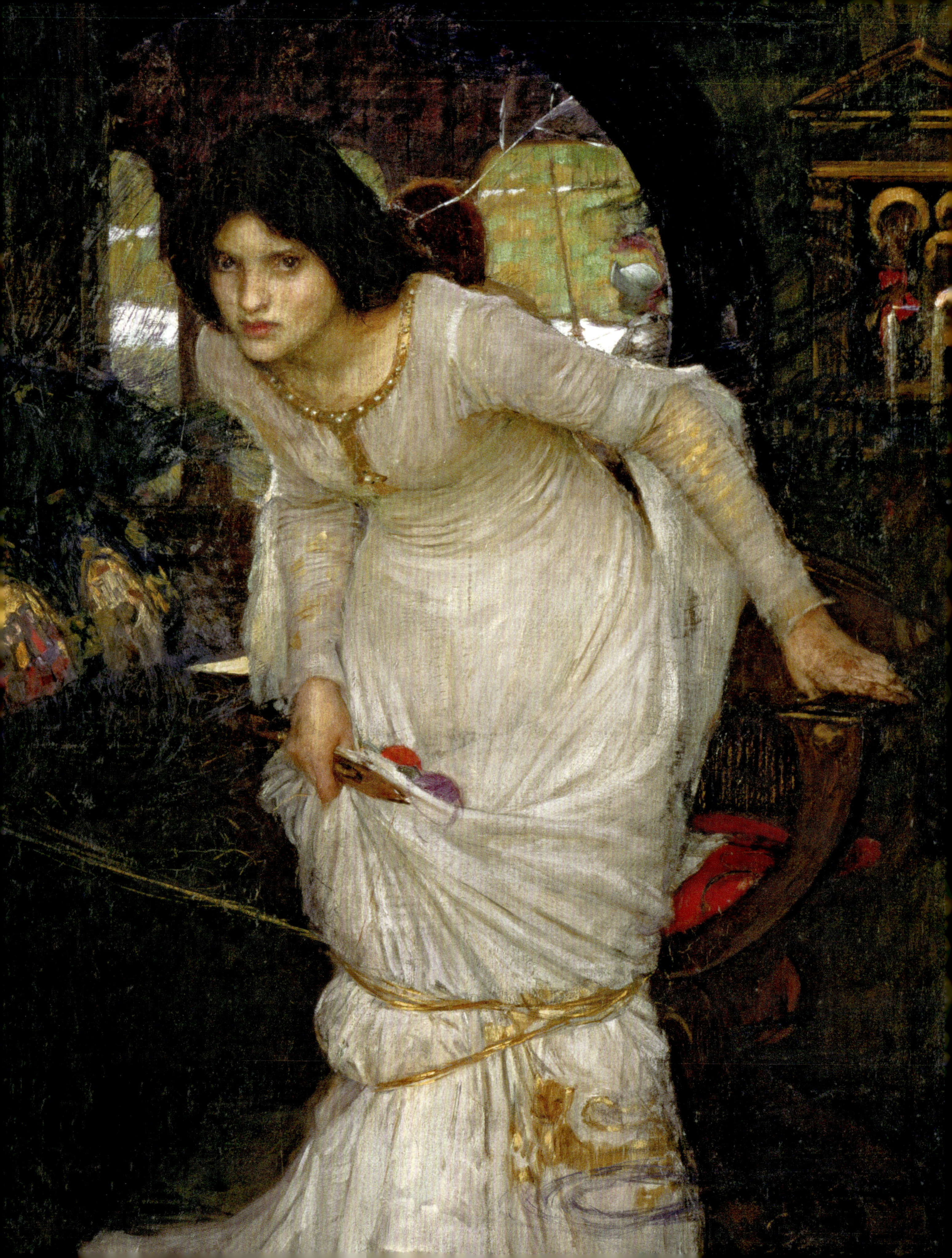

THE LADY OF SHALOTT

Alfred, Lord Tennyson (1809–1892)

Part I

On either side the river lie
Long fields of barley and of rye,
That clothe the wold and meet the sky;
And thro' the field the road runs by
To many-tower'd Camelot;
And up and down the people go,
Gazing where the lilies blow
Round an island there below,
The island of Shalott.

Willows whiten, aspens quiver,
Little breezes dusk and shiver
Thro' the wave that runs for ever
By the island in the river
Flowing down to Camelot.
Four gray walls, and four gray towers,
Overlook a space of flowers,
And the silent isle imbowers
The Lady of Shalott.

By the margin, willow-veil'd,
Slide the heavy barges trail'd
By slow horses; and unhail'd
The shallop flitteth silken-sail'd
Skimming down to Camelot:
But who hath seen her wave her hand?
Or at the casement seen her stand?
Or is she known in all the land,
The Lady of Shalott?

Only reapers, reaping early
In among the bearded barley,
Hear a song that echoes cheerly
From the river winding clearly,
Down to tower'd Camelot:
And by the moon the reaper weary,
Piling sheaves in uplands airy,
Listening, whispers ''Tis the fairy
Lady of Shalott.'

Part II

There she weaves by night and day
A magic web with colours gay.
She has heard a whisper say,
A curse is on her if she stay
To look down to Camelot.
She knows not what the curse may be,
And so she weaveth steadily,
And little other care hath she,
The Lady of Shalott.

And moving thro' a mirror clear
That hangs before her all the year,
Shadows of the world appear.
There she sees the highway near
Winding down to Camelot:
There the river eddy whirls,
And there the surly village-churls,
And the red cloaks of market girls,
Pass onward from Shalott.

Sometimes a troop of damsels glad,
An abbot on an ambling pad,
Sometimes a curly shepherd-lad,
Or long-hair'd page in crimson clad,
Goes by to tower'd Camelot;
And sometimes thro' the mirror blue
The knights come riding two and two:
She hath no loyal knight and true,
The Lady of Shalott.

But in her web she still delights
To weave the mirror's magic sights,
For often thro' the silent nights
A funeral, with plumes and lights,
And music, went to Camelot:
Or when the moon was overhead,
Came two young lovers lately wed;
'I am half sick of shadows,' said
The Lady of Shalott.

Part III

A bow-shot from her bower-eaves,
He rode between the barley-sheaves,
The sun came dazzling thro' the leaves,
And flamed upon the brazen greaves
Of bold Sir Lancelot.
A red-cross knight for ever kneel'd
To a lady in his shield,
That sparkled on the yellow field,
Beside remote Shalott.

The gemmy bridle glitter'd free,
Like to some branch of stars we see
Hung in the golden Galaxy.
The bridle bells rang merrily
As he rode down to Camelot:
And from his blazon'd baldric slung
A mighty silver bugle hung,
And as he rode his armour rung,
Beside remote Shalott.

All in the blue unclouded weather
Thick-jewell'd shone the saddle-leather,
The helmet and the helmet-feather
Burn'd like one burning flame together,
As he rode down to Camelot.
As often thro' the purple night,
Below the starry clusters bright,
Some bearded meteor, trailing light,
Moves over still Shalott.

His broad clear brow in sunlight glow'd;
On burnish'd hooves his war-horse trode;
From underneath his helmet flow'd
His coal-black curls as on he rode,
　　As he rode down to Camelot.
From the bank and from the river
He flash'd into the crystal mirror,
'Tirra lirra,' by the river
　　Sang Sir Lancelot.

She left the web, she left the loom,
She made three paces thro' the room,
She saw the water-lily bloom,
She saw the helmet and the plume,
　　She look'd down to Camelot.
Out flew the web and floated wide;
The mirror crack'd from side to side;
'The curse is come upon me!' cried
　　The Lady of Shalott.

Part IV

In the stormy east-wind straining,
The pale yellow woods were waning,
The broad stream in his banks
complaining,
Heavily the low sky raining
　　Over tower'd Camelot;
Down she came and found a boat
Beneath a willow left afloat,
And round about the prow she wrote
　　The Lady of Shalott.

And down the river's dim expanse—
Like some bold seer in a trance,
Seeing all his own mischance—
With a glassy countenance
　　Did she look to Camelot.
And at the closing of the day
She loosed the chain, and down she lay;
The broad stream bore her far away,
　　The Lady of Shalott.

Lying, robed in snowy white
That loosely flew to left and right—
The leaves upon her falling light—
Thro' the noises of the night
　　She floated down to Camelot:
And as the boat-head wound along
The willowy hills and fields among,
They heard her singing her last song,
　　The Lady of Shalott.

Heard a carol, mournful, holy,
Chanted loudly, chanted lowly,
Till her blood was frozen slowly,
And her eyes were darken'd wholly,
　　Turn'd to tower'd Camelot;
For ere she reach'd upon the tide
The first house by the water-side,
Singing in her song she died,
　　The Lady of Shalott.

Under tower and balcony,
By garden-wall and gallery,
A gleaming shape she floated by,
Dead-pale between the houses high,
　　Silent into Camelot.
Out upon the wharfs they came,
Knight and burgher, lord and dame,
And round the prow they read her name,
　　The Lady of Shalott.

Who is this? and what is here?
And in the lighted palace near
Died the sound of royal cheer;
And they cross'd themselves for fear,
　　All the knights at Camelot:
But Lancelot mused a little space;
He said, 'She has a lovely face;
God in His mercy lend her grace,
　　The Lady of Shalott.'

Previous page: Fig. 16, detail of Cat. 32, p. 60
Right: Fig. 17, detail of Cat. 33, p. 61

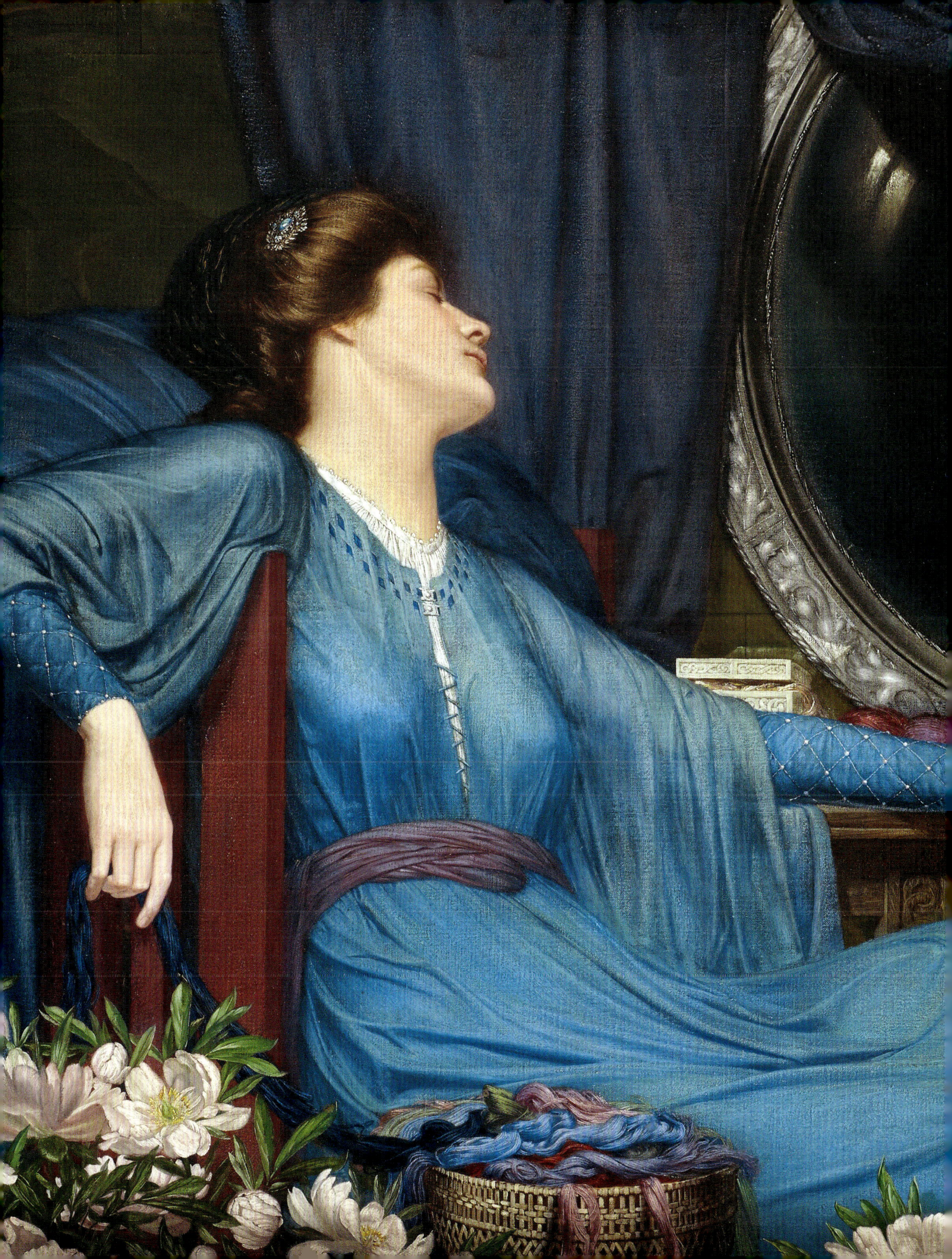

PICTURE NOTES

Caroline Bugler

Edward Burne-Jones (1833–1898)
Sketchbook, with drawings of decorative details, some from the *Ghent Altarpiece* by Hubert and Jan van Eyck, after 1859
Pencil and watercolour on paper (bound volume; in leather), 19.1 × 26.4 cm
Victoria and Albert Museum, London. Given by Dr W.L. Hildburgh F.S.A (E.4-1955)

From the middle of the nineteenth century coloured reproductions of van Eyck's *Ghent Altarpiece* began to circulate in Britain. Burne-Jones probably made the two central studies on this sheet from a chromolithograph, since he never travelled to Ghent to experience the altarpiece at first hand, unlike his friends Morris, Rossetti and Hunt. One drawing shows the hands of van Eyck's Virgin Mary holding a book, the other shows her crown, and both are carefully annotated with notes on colour. The artist may have referred to the study of the crown when he was designing his *Adoration of the Magi* tapestry (1890), woven by Morris & Co. for Exeter College, Oxford, since it features an almost identical crown. p. 21

Dante Gabriel Rossetti (1828–1882)
The Girlhood of Mary Virgin, 1848–9
Oil on canvas, 83.2 × 65.4 cm
Tate, London. Bequeathed by Lady Jekyll 1937 (N04872)

This was the first Pre-Raphaelite painting to appear in public with the group's secret initials, PRB. It was dedicated to the Virgin Mary as a symbol of female excellence as described in the sonnet on the bottom of the frame. The Virgin is shown embroidering the lily held by an angel under the guidance of her mother, Saint Anne. Rossetti's mother Frances and sister Christina posed for the figures of Saint Anne and the Virgin; the strong element of realistic portraiture in their faces stands out against the medieval setting. The painting is filled with symbolic allusions: the palm branch and thorn on the floor refer to Christ's Passion; the lily to the Virgin's purity; the books to the virtues of Faith, Hope and Charity; and the dove sitting on the vine pruned by the Virgin's father, Joachim, to the Holy Spirit. The anti-perspectival structure of the room, the minute application of colour and the symbolic treatment of objects may all have been suggested by the *Arnolfini Portrait*. p. 34

John Everett Millais (1829–1896)
Mrs James Wyatt Jr and her Daughter Sarah, about 1850
Oil on mahogany panel, 35.3 × 45.7 cm
Tate, London. Purchased 1984 (T03858)

James Wyatt, an Oxford art dealer and print publisher, was one of Millais's early patrons, and commissioned the artist to paint a portrait of himself with his granddaughter, Mary, in 1849. This double portrait of Wyatt's daughter-in-law, Eliza, and her daughter is its pendant. On the wall behind the figures is a print of Leonardo's *Last Supper* flanked by Raphael's *Madonna della Sedia* and *Alba Madonna*. As a Pre-Raphaelite, Millais detested Raphael's soft and idealised depictions of mother and child, and his own interpretation of the theme is sharply focused, stark and realistic. The stiffness of the figures is also reminiscent of the poses of early daguerreotype portraits. When this portrait was hung next to its companion a further comparison could have been made: on the wall above James Wyatt's head is a more conventionally romantic portrait of Eliza by Sir William Boxall, whose circular shape recalls the *tondo* format of Raphael's two Madonnas. p. 36

John Everett Millais (1829–1896)
Mariana, 1851
Oil on mahogany, 59.7 × 49.5 cm
Tate, London. Accepted by HM Government in lieu of tax and allocated to the Tate Gallery 1999 (T07553)

Mariana in the Moated Grange, 1850
Pen and ink on paper, 21.5 × 12.9 cm
Victoria and Albert Museum, London (E.354-1931)

Mariana, who appears in Shakespeare's *Measure for Measure* and in a poem by Tennyson, has been sent into exile by her fiancé Angelo after her dowry was lost at sea. When Millais showed *Mariana* at the Royal Academy in 1851 he included the refrain from Tennyson's poem as if to emphasise the protagonist's melancholy in captivity:

She only said, 'My life is dreary –
He cometh not' she said;
She said, 'I am aweary, aweary –
I would that I were dead!'

Mariana's pose, back arched and hands on hips, is frankly erotic, and the stained glass featuring the Annunciation and a lily, symbolic of purity, seems like an ironic commentary on her unfulfilled longing for her lover. Leaves from the outside world have blown in to settle on the floral embroidery, emphasising Mariana's isolation from nature.
An earlier pen and ink study for the composition indicates that Millais was originally thinking of including a round mirror behind Mariana's head, perhaps reflecting her loosened hair. pp. 40 and 41

William Holman Hunt (1827–1910)
The Awakening Conscience, 1853–4
Oil on canvas 76.2 × 55.9 cm
Tate, London. Presented by Sir Colin and Lady Anderson through the Friends of the Tate Gallery 1976 (T02075)

Hunt exhibited this painting at the Royal Academy in 1854. He conceived it as a pendant to his earlier *Light of the World,* a nocturnal scene showing Christ knocking at a door intended to represent the human soul. It portrays a kept mistress's moment of moral awakening as she rises from the lap of the wealthy lover. The claustrophobic interior is filled with furniture notable for what Ruskin described as 'a fatal newness', and every detail amplifies the narrative: the woman appears to be in a state of semi-undress; she is not wearing a wedding ring; the music on the piano is Thomas Moore's 'Oft in the Stilly Night', which has perhaps reminded her of lost innocence; and on the floor lies the setting of Tennyson's poem 'Tears, Idle Tears'. The bird trying to escape from the cat under the table, the single discarded glove and the unravelling skeins of wool allude to the woman's uncertain future, which depends on her lover's fickle affections. Yet the sunlit garden reflected in the mirror behind her suggests that she will choose a path towards spiritual enlightenment, and that faith will be her salvation. p. 42

Ford Madox Brown (1821–1893)
'Take your Son, Sir', begun 1851–2, enlarged and reworked 1856–7
Oil on canvas, 70.5 × 38.1 cm
Tate, London. Presented by Miss Emily Sargent and Mrs Ormond in memory of their brother John S. Sargent 1929 (N04429)

Brown began this painting as a portrait of his mistress, Emma, whom he married in 1853. He later enlarged and transformed it into an image of motherhood, the circular mirror serving as a kind of halo. Yet this is far from a conventional picture of mother and child: the woman looks flushed and exhausted rather than serene, and the narrative context is far from clear. The words on the canvas imply that she is exhorting her husband, who is seen reflected in the mirror, to hold their son so he can be dressed in his nightshirt; just visible on the right-hand side a maid is preparing a cot for the baby. He is the couple's third son, Arthur Gabriel, who was born in 1856, and the painting may be a celebration of the birth since Brown himself is the father shown in the mirror. Arthur died the following year, and the artist's grief at the loss led him to abandon the picture. p. 45

William Morris (1834–1896)
La Belle Iseult, 1857–8
Oil on canvas, 71.8 × 50.2 cm
Tate, London. Bequeathed by Miss May Morris 1939 (N04999)

The subject of Morris's only known easel painting derives from Malory's version of the legend of Tristram and Iseult. It shows Iseult – modelled by Jane Burden, whom Morris married in 1859 – alone in her chamber following her lover Tristram's exile from court. The girdle she fastens around her waist suggests her enforced chastity, while the sprig of rosemary in her crown symbolises remembrance, the convolvulus the couple's attachment, and the word 'DOLOURS' (meaning grief) written down the side of the mirror reinforces the sense of melancholy. The bed, carpet, oranges, dog, mirror and slipper are all derived from the *Arnolfini Portrait*, as are Iseult's pose and the sheer perspective of the room, which contributes to the sense of her confinement. Morris experienced considerable trouble with the portrait element of the picture, and according to contemporary reports abandoned the canvas as unfinished. The carefully observed objects and textiles reflect his interest in the decorative arts and the value he placed on craftsmanship. p. 46

Edward Burne-Jones (1833–1898)
Fair Rosamund and Queen Eleanor, 1862
Ink, watercolour, gouache and gum on paper, 26 × 27.3 cm
Tate, London. Presented by J.R. Holliday through the Art Fund 1923 (N03822)

One of seven studies for Fair Rosamund and Queen Eleanor, about 1862
Pencil on paper, 24.6 × 22 cm
Victoria and Albert Museum, London. Bequeathed by J.R. Holliday (E.2857-1927)

According to legend, King Henry II created a hidden chamber for his mistress, Rosamund, at the centre of an elaborate maze. She was discovered and murdered there by her rival, Queen Eleanor, who followed a red cord to find her. In 1859 Burne-Jones visited Godstowe, where Rosamund was said to have been buried, in the company of Algernon Swinburne. The poet was inspired to write a verse drama that probably formed the basis for the artist's visual interpretations, which he explored in several versions painted in the early 1860s. The circular mirror is based on one made by the artist's father, but ultimately derives from that in van Eyck's *Arnolfini Portrait*. Each separate roundel picks up a different aspect of the Queen's profile as she approaches her victim, whose attempts to flee are impeded by the cord. In the pencil study for the mirror Burne-Jones explores different angles of Queen Eleanor's profile as reflected in each roundel. The idea of fragmentation and rotation is simplified in the finished painting. p. 48 and p. 50

Edward Burne-Jones (1833–1898)
Study for St Valentine's Day, verso of Study for 'The Merciful Knight', about 1863
Graphite on paper, 25.8 × 17.8 cm
Tate, London. Bequeathed by J.R. Holliday 1927 (A00084)

In the early 1860s Burne-Jones made watercolours based on British folklore and legend. This study for a now lost watercolour uses a convex mirror for dramatic effect. The reflection shows the outline of a maid preparing a wedding breakfast, and the mirror doubles up as the morning sun revealed by the winged figure of Love as he bursts through the window, surprising the woman in bed. In the finished watercolour the position of the mirror and the window are reversed. p. 50

Dante Gabriel Rossetti (1828–1882)
Lucrezia Borgia, 1860–1
Graphite and watercolour on paper, 43.8 × 25.8 cm
Tate, London. Presented in memory of Henry Michael Field by Charles Ricketts though the Art Fund 1916 (NG03063)

Rossetti's choice of this subject was no doubt influenced by his friend Algernon Swinburne, who was writing a book about the infamous Renaissance figure Lucrezia Borgia at the time. The artist was also embarking on a series of bust-length paintings of beautiful women that reflected his admiration for the Venetian Old Masters and celebrated powerful sexuality rather than purity and modesty. Here the female protagonist is an archetypal *femme fatale*, who poisoned her husband,

Duke Alfonso Bisceglie, aided by her father, Pope Alexander VI, who no longer found the marital alliance to his advantage. The reflection in the mirror shows him helping the Duke to walk in order to spread the poison through his whole body. The murderess looks calmly towards the viewer while washing her hands. Inspired by Rossetti's example, Burne-Jones started to employ circular mirrors to explore sinister themes, as in *Fair Rosamund and Queen Eleanor* (cats 21, 22). p. 51

Simeon Solomon (1840–1905)

A Youth relating Tales to Ladies, 1870

Oil on canvas, 35.5 × 53.4 cm

Tate, London. Presented by the Kretschmer family in accordance with the wishes of William Kretchmer 1983 (T03702)

This is one of a number of works that Simeon Solomon painted in the 1870s featuring frieze-like arrangements of figures in shallow space. In keeping with the aims of the Aesthetic movement, of which Solomon was a key exponent, the emphasis is on formal qualities and introspection rather than narrative. A group of women in vaguely Regency dress are shown listening to a story related by a young man. There is no hint as to what the tale might be, although the mood is one of poetic lassitude – indeed when the painting was first exhibited one reviewer remarked that 'these "tales" could not have sparkled with wit'. The small circular mirror in the background is the type that would have been seen in fashionable interiors of the period, but its obscure reflection, which may show an easel and canvas but no artist, serves to echo the dreamy mood of the painting rather than opening up space. p. 53

Henry Treffry Dunn (1838–1899)

Dante Gabriel Rossetti's Bedroom at Tudor House, 16 Cheyne Walk, 1872

Watercolour on paper, 33.5 × 33.5 cm

Wightwick Manor, the National Trust. Given to the National Trust by Mrs. Helen Annie Handford Guglielmini in 2001 (Inv. 1287978)

Rossetti moved to Tudor House at 16 Cheyne Walk after the death of his wife, furnishing it in his own unique style and installing a menagerie of exotic animals. Over the two decades he spent there he gradually became more depressed and reclusive. Henry Treffry Dunn, Rossetti's personal secretary and studio assistant, painted this ingenious picture of the artist's bedroom as seen in one of the many convex mirrors in the house, the shadowy and distorted reflection conveying an overwhelming sense of claustrophobia. It shows the four-poster bed and the overmantel crowded with the blue-and-white porcelain that was a key element in many Aesthetic interiors. Dunn thought the bedroom 'a most unhealthy place to sleep', mentioning 'Thick curtains heavy with crewel work in designs of print and foliage hung closely drawn round an antiquated four-post bedstead' and the additional clutter of bronze 'Chinese monstrosities' and vases filled with peacock feathers and brass repoussé dishes. p. 53

William Holman Hunt (1827–1910)

Il Dolce far Niente, 1859–66, reworked 1874–5

Oil on canvas, 99.1 × 80 cm

Private Collection

Unusually for Hunt, this is a painting with no didactic purpose or narrative. Its Italian title means 'It is sweet to do nothing', and it is simply a celebration of female beauty of the type that Hunt's contemporaries, Frederic Leighton and Rossetti, were producing at the time. The original model was Annie Miller, whom Hunt planned to wed, but after the engagement was broken off he substituted the face of Fanny Waugh, whom he married in 1865. The woman's tumbling locks and the richly textured dress breathe sensuality, but she is wearing an engagement ring, which implies respectability. There is much to suggest the warmth of a permanent home unlike the hastily assembled household depicted in *The Awakening Conscience* (cat. 18). The reflection in the circular mirror – which bears little spatial relationship to the scene in front of it – reveals a fire, evoking cosy domesticity. The 'Egyptian' style chair in which the woman sits is one Hunt commissioned for his own home. p. 55

Elizabeth Eleanor Siddall (1829–1862)

The Lady of Shalott, 1853

Pen, ink and pencil on paper, 24.8 × 17.8 cm

The Maas Gallery

Elizabeth Eleanor Siddall's pencil drawing presents her own interpretation of the popular *Lady of Shalott* theme, showing the moment when the lady turns away from her loom to glance out of the window towards Sir Lancelot, who she could previously only see in a reflection in her circular mirror. The consequences of her move, which will bring about her eventual death, are implicit in the threads bursting out of the tapestry frame and the cracks that have appeared in the mirror. Unlike the Ladies of Shalott depicted by Hunt (cat. 31) and Waterhouse (cat. 32), Siddall's protagonist is decidedly asexual, dressed in a plain robe and devoid of sensuous curves. p. 57

William Holman Hunt (1827–1910)
The Lady of Shalott, engraved by J. Thompson, published 1857
Wood engraving on paper, 9.5 × 7.9 cm
Tate, London. Presented by Harold Hartley 1925 (N04052)

In 1857 Hunt was commissioned to design an illustration for *The Lady of Shalott* for Edward Moxon's collection of Tennyson's poems. This shows the lady with wild outflung hair struggling with the threads of the loom in front of an enormous van Eyck-inspired mirror. The engraving served as the template for the oil version of the same subject that he painted almost 30 years later. p. 58

William Holman Hunt (1827–1910)
The Lady of Shalott, about 1886–1905
Oil on wood, 44.4 × 34.1 cm
Manchester City Art Gallery (1934.401)

Hunt's representation of the Lady of Shalott illustrates the fateful lines in Tennyson's poem when the lady sees Sir Lancelot advancing towards Camelot in her mirror, and cannot resist the urge to look out of the window at the real world:

'Out flew the web and floated wide;
The mirror crack'd from side to side;
"The curse is come upon me!" cried
The Lady of Shalott.'

Based on Hunt's earlier engraving for Moxon's *Tennyson* (cat. 30), the design also recalls his *Awakening Conscience* (cat. 18), in which a mirror reflects a moment of revelation. The lady's outflung hair echoes the threads of the tapestry that unravel in the foreground, and the turmoil causes two doves to scatter. The circular mirror and wooden pattens are objects seen in the *Arnolfini Portrait*, and the silver samovar topped with candles is a reference to van Eyck's brass chandelier. Two ovals either side of the mirror depict Christ in Majesty and the Agony of Christ in the Garden, underlining the moral implications of a painting that Hunt saw as symbolising the failure of an artist to carry out duties because he or she is distracted by personal desires. p. 59

John William Waterhouse (1849–1917)
The Lady of Shalott, 1894
Oil on canvas, 142.2 × 86.3 cm
Leeds Museums and Galleries (Leeds Art Gallery, LEEAG.1895.0004)

Waterhouse painted a number of versions of the *The Lady of Shalott* that were influenced by the earlier Pre-Raphaelite paintings being displayed again in public at large retrospective exhibitions of the artists' works in the 1880s. Here he depicts the moment in Tennyson's poem when the lady imprisoned in her tower turns away from the mirror that reflects the outside world and looks out of the window at Sir Lancelot, thereby unleashing the fatal curse. This painting recalls Hunt's depiction of the subject (cat. 31), and the devotional altar looks like the one in Millais's *Mariana* (cat. 16). Waterhouse's 1888 version of *The Lady of Shalott* (Tate) depicts a later stage in the narrative when the lady drifts downstream to Camelot in a boat, and his 1915 painting on the theme (Art Gallery of Ontario, Toronto) shows the melancholy lady at her tapestry frame. p. 60

Sidney Meteyard (1868–1947)
'I am Half-Sick of Shadows, Said the Lady of Shalott', 1913
Oil on canvas, 76 × 114.5 cm
Private Collection, courtesy of Martin Beisly

Meteyard's painting in a late Pre-Raphaelite manner illustrates a point in Tennyson's poem when the lady, wearied at the sight of 'two young lovers lately wed' seen in the magic mirror, closes her eyes to its shadowy reflection. Her languorous pose and the mass of flowers in the foreground accentuate the eroticism of the moment. The painting's rich colour may reflect Meteyard's experience of working in stained glass and enamel. The enamel plaques he produced with his wife Kate Eadie (who modelled for the lady) are further echoed in the embroidery, which features a knight on horseback, anticipating the imminent arrival of Lancelot. The general treatment looks back to the paintings of the theme by Hunt and Waterhouse, while the mirror is ultimately derived from van Eyck via similar examples in the work of Hunt and Burne-Jones. p. 61

Edward Burne-Jones (1833–1898)
Margaret Burne-Jones, 1885–6
Oil on canvas, 91.2 × 66 cm
Private Collection

Burne-Jones's adored daughter Margaret stands in front of the open door of her bedroom, which can be glimpsed in the convex mirror behind her. She was 19 or 20 at the time and possessed the type of classical beauty the artist particularly admired. The large mirror behind her head forms a kind of halo and echoes her round reflective eyes, while the impression of purity and innocence is reinforced by the blue of her dress – the colour associated with the Virgin Mary. Not long after the portrait was painted Margaret married J.W. Mackail, a man of letters and a friend of William Morris, and Burne-Jones felt terrible pangs of jealousy at the prospect of sharing her company with a man he knew primarily as a scholar. p. 63

Charles Shannon (1863–1937)
The Bath of Venus, 1898–1904
Oil on canvas, 146 × 97.8 cm
Tate, London. Presented by Francis Howard 1940 (N05160)

Shannon took six years to complete this picture, which shows the Roman goddess Venus in her bath with attendants, its luscious sensuality evoking the mood of Rossetti's paintings of women. It was originally called *The Green Marble Bath*, but Shannon later changed it to *The Bath of Venus*, the title used for a similar composition by Burne-Jones in a painting of 1873–8 (now lost). The new title also deliberately suggests subjects chosen by Old Masters such as Titian, who was enjoying a revival of interest at the end of the nineteenth century, as well as the classical statuary that had inspired Titian. Above the enclosed world of the bath, the circular mirror reflects the backs of the attendants and echoes the reflections seen in the water, basin and ewer. p. 64

Charles Shannon (1863–1937)
Les Marmitons, 1897
Oil on canvas on board, 39 × 36.6 cm
Tate, London. Purchased 1942 (N05363)

Shannon's picture shows two girls in seventeenth-century costume, who have donned fancy dress to disguise themselves as *'marmitons'* – male kitchen servants. They gaze out at the viewer who appears to have interrupted their game of make-believe, the reflections of their backs that flash up in the circular mirror behind them playing on the idea of doubling and disguise, while the haziness conveys the transitory nature of the moment. p. 65

John Phillip (1817–1867)
Partial copy of 'Las Meninas', 1862
Oil on canvas, 185 × 148 cm
Royal Academy of Arts, London (03/1097)

Diego Velázquez (1599–1660) admired the *Arnolfini Portrait*, which belonged to the Spanish Royal Collection during the time he was a court artist, and his own *Las Meninas* (1656, see p. 15) also plays with the notion of the image reflected in a mirror to create a puzzling ambiguity. John Phillip's partial copy of the Spanish master's most celebrated work eliminates the right-hand side of the picture, thus placing the mirror, which reflects the King and Queen of Spain, in the middle of the canvas rather than on the left. The picture hung in the Diploma Galleries at the Royal Academy from 1868, where it was seen by many artists and students. By that time the first phase of Pre-Raphaelitism was over, and a number of its adherents had moved on to embrace the broader treatment and dark tonality of Old Masters such as Velázquez that they had previously found abhorrent. p. 68

Wolfram Onslow Ford (1879–1956)
My Father, reproduction of the missing original printed in *The Studio*, vol. 25, 1902
Tate Archives, London (35885–1001)

This photograph of a missing portrait depicts the artist's father, the sculptor Edward Onslow Ford (1852–1901), in his studio. Although it was painted in 1899, half a century after the foundation of the Pre-Raphaelite Brotherhood, it shows the close attention to symbolic detail seen in their early works. Edward Onslow Ford was a founding member of the Art Workers Guild, which sought to bring together painters, sculptors and decorative artists and promote craft practices, and the picture sums up his artistic philosophy. He holds a reproduction of the *Arnolfini Portrait*, which displays the craftsmanship and realism he admired, and the convex mirror on the wall is a direct homage to van Eyck's painting. In the background are the sculptor's polychrome statuette *The Singer* (1889), which shows a girl harpist with an Egyptian headdress standing on an Egyptian pedestal, and his *Shelley Memorial* (1892), for which his son was the model. p. 69

William Orpen (1878–1931)
The Mirror, 1900
Oil on canvas, 50.8 × 40.6 cm
Tate, London. Presented by Mrs Coutts Michie through the Art Fund in memory of the George McCulloch Collection 1913 (N02940)

William Orpen was briefly engaged to the sitter, Emily Scoble, who was a model at the Slade School of Art. She is shown in front of the circular mirror in the artist's studio. While the seated pose, restricted palette and shallow depth recall Whistler's famous portrait of his mother, the mirror is a direct reference to the *Arnolfini Portrait*. It reflects the image of the artist at work at his easel, with another woman, who is not identified, at his side. The room is furnished with canvases and framed paintings, and in place of van Eyck's brass candelabra we see a crystal chandelier and a lamp. p. 71

William Orpen (1878–1931)
A Bloomsbury Family, 1907
Oil on canvas, 86.5 × 91.5 cm
Scottish National Gallery of Modern Art, Edinburgh (GMA 881)

The painting shows the artist William Nicholson, his wife Mabel Pryde, who was also a painter, and their four children in their dining room in Mecklenburgh Square, Bloomsbury. The room is shrouded in shadow, the brightest spot of light provided by the window seen in the convex mirror, in which Orpen's own reflection can just be made out. As in *The Mirror* (Cat. 40), the artist shows himself seated at an easel with a female figure by his side. The mirror itself is ultimately derived from the *Arnolfini Portrait* and the Pre-Raphaelites. Sitting at the table from left to right are Nancy, who married the writer Robert Graves; Tony, who died during the war in 1918; and Ben, who became an important pioneer of abstract art. The young boy standing in the foreground is Christopher or 'Kit', who became an architect; he is clothed in a type of frock often worn by young boys at the time. p. 72

Arthur Studd (1863–1919)
Self Portrait in a Round Mirror, early twentieth century
Pencil on paper, 13 × 11.5 cm
Private Collection

Studd's pencil drawing – a hazy monochrome image resembling a faded photograph – depicts a circular mirror hanging on the wall, which reflects the artist at work in an elegant interior and the presence of a further overmantel mirror in the background. Studd was a friend of Whistler and owned his *Symphony in White No. 2: The Little White Girl* painted in 1864 (Tate), which shows a young woman gazing at her own reflection in a mirror. At the time he painted his picture Whistler was on friendly terms with the Pre-Raphaelites, and would probably have seen such works as Hunt's *Awakening Conscience*. Whistler's painting, in turn, may well have prompted Studd's small sketch. p. 73

Mark Gertler (1891–1939)
Still Life with Self Portrait, 1918
Oil on canvas, 50.8 × 40.6 cm
Leeds Museums and Galleries (Leeds Art Gallery, LEEAG.1956.0001.0003)

Virginia Woolf, who met Mark Gertler at around the time he painted this canvas, described his face as 'a little tight and pinched; but the word he would wish one to use of him is powerful. His mind certainly has a powerful spring to it. He is also evidently an immense egoist.' Interested in his own image, Gertler produced a number of self portraits, but none have the spatial complexity of this work in which he is seen in the convex mirror. The reflection reveals that he is painting the still life arranged in front of the mirror; the details of his studio are compressed into the distorted space behind him. The shiny surface of the bottle and the brass candlestick – perhaps an echo of the Arnolfini candelabra – gleam with further reflections. A menacing samurai figure in the Japanese print behind the mirror looks as though it is about to strike at the artist's image, implying some impending threat. Gertler admired Dutch seventeenth-century still-life paintings, which often contain reminders of death. p. 74

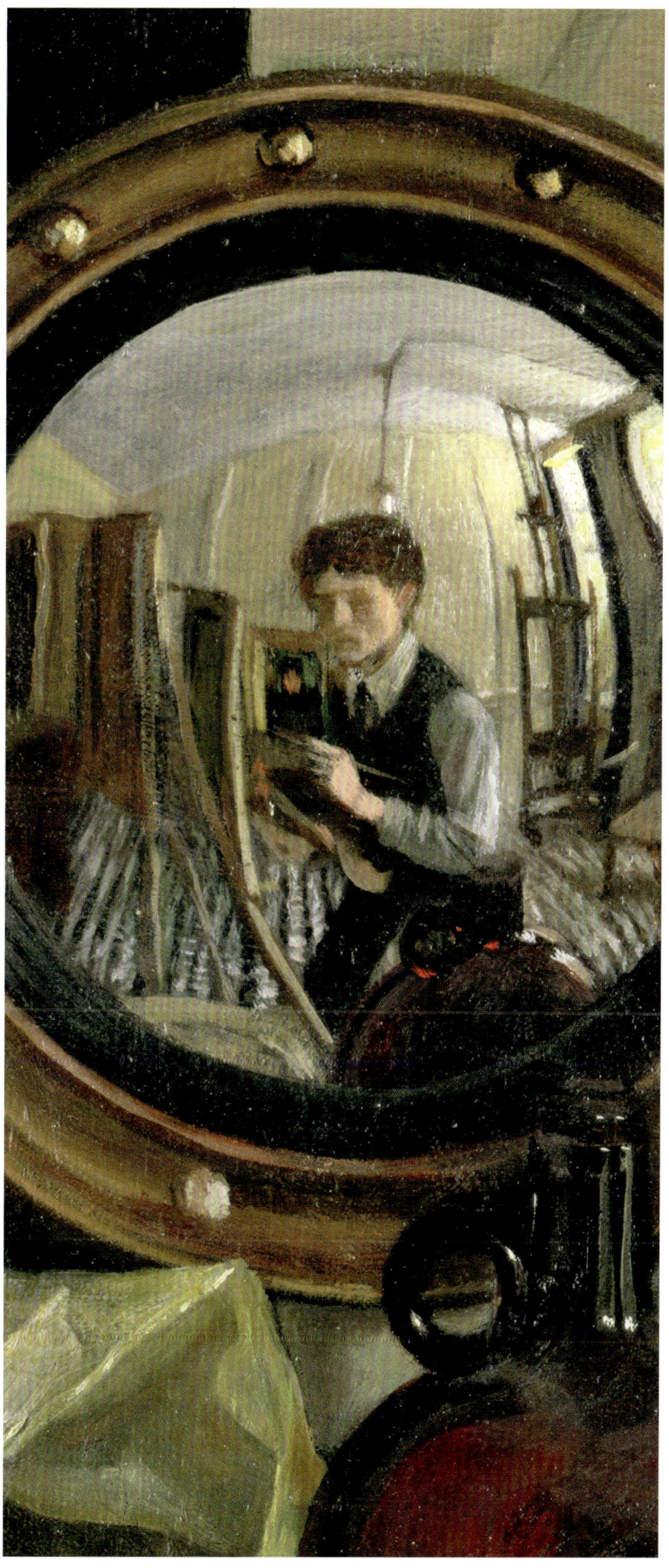

Fig. 18, detail of cat. 43, p. 74

LIST OF EXHIBITED WORKS

Cat. 1

Jan van Eyck (active 1422; died 1441)

Portrait of Giovanni(?) Arnolfini and his Wife (The Arnolfini Portrait), 1434

Oil on oak, 82.2 × 60 cm

The National Gallery, London. Bought, 1842 (NG 186)

Cat. 2

Jan van Eyck (active 1422; died 1441)

Portrait of a Man (Self Portrait?), 1433

Oil on oak, 26 × 19 cm;

The National Gallery, London. Bought, 1851 (NG 222)

Cat. 3

Memorandum written by James Wardrop, 1865

The National Gallery Archive, London (NGA0/4/2/228)

Cat. 4

Treasury letter, dated May 2 1842, stating that the Lords would recommend to Parliament the purchase of the *Arnolfini Portrait.*

The National Gallery Archive, London (NG5/50/1)

Cat. 5

The Illustrated London News, April 1843

Bound volume (Jan–June 1843)

Museum of London (74.335/1)

Cat. 6

Woodcut of the *Arnolfini Portrait* by the Linnell brothers, on page 49 of *Felix Summerly's Handbook for the National Gallery.* London: G. Bell, 1843.

The National Gallery Library, London (109455)

Cat. 7

Dirk Bouts (1400?–1475)

Christ Crowned with Thorns, about 1470

Oil with egg tempera on canvas backed onto board, transferred from wood, 43.8 × 37.1 cm

The National Gallery, London. Bequeathed by Mrs Joseph H. Green, 1880 (NG 1083)

Cat. 8

Hans Memling (active 1465; died 1494)

The Virgin and Child with an Angel, Saint George and a Donor, about 1480

Oil on oak, 54.2 × 37.4 cm

The National Gallery, London. Bought, 1862 (NG 686)

Cat. 9

Reproduction of the *Ghent Altarpiece* by Hubert van Eyck (died 1426) and Jan van Eyck (active 1422; died 1441), 1868–71

Chromolithograph plates in a black frame, 150 × 100 cm

The Maas Gallery

Cat. 10

Edward Burne-Jones (1833–1898)

Sketchbook, with drawings of decorative details, some from the *Ghent Altarpiece* by Hubert and Jan van Eyck, after 1859

Pencil and watercolour on paper (bound volume; in leather), 19.1 × 26.4 cm

Victoria and Albert Museum, London Given by Dr W.L. Hildburgh, F.S.A (E.4-1955)

Cat. 11

Laubier, Paris

Léo François Louis de Mestral and his wife Léonie de Banes de Gardonne, about 1856

Gold-toned daguerreotype, 9.4 × 7 cm

Wilson Centre for Photography, London (12:1418)

Cat. 12

Anonymous photographer (thought to be in London)

Portrait of two Women, about 1845

Daguerreotype, 8.7 × 6.7 cm

Wilson Centre for Photography, London (84:1193)

Cat. 13

Dante Gabriel Rossetti (1828–1882)

The Girlhood of Mary Virgin, 1848–9

Oil on canvas, 83.2 × 63.4 cm

Tate, London. Bequeathed by Lady Jekyll 1937 (N04872)

Cat. 14

John Everett Millais (1829–1896)

Mrs James Wyatt Jr and her Daughter Sarah, about 1850

Oil on mahogany panel, 35.3 × 45.7 cm

Tate, London. Purchased 1984 (T03858)

Cat. 15

Antoine Claudet (1797–1867)

Two Boys, thought to be Brothers, about 1855

Hand-tinted stereo daguerreotype, gold-toned, 6.7 × 5.7 cm

Wilson Centre for Photography, London (11:1312)

Cat. 16

John Everett Millais (1829–1896)

Mariana, 1851

Oil on mahogany, 59.7 × 49.5 cm

Tate, London. Accepted by HM Government in lieu of tax and allocated to the Tate Gallery 1999 (T07553)

Cat. 17

John Everett Millais (1829–1896)

Mariana in the Moated Grange, 1850

Pen and ink on paper, 21.5 × 12.9 cm

Victoria and Albert Museum, London (E.354-1931)

Cat. 18

William Holman Hunt (1827–1910)

The Awakening Conscience, 1853

Oil on canvas, 76.2 × 55.9 cm

Tate, London. Presented by Sir Colin and Lady Anderson through the Friends of the Tate Gallery 1976 (T02075)

Cat. 19

Ford Madox Brown (1821–1893)

'Take your Son, Sir!', begun 1851–2, enlarged and reworked 1856–7

Oil on canvas, 70.5 × 38.1 cm

Tate, London. Presented by Miss Emily Sargent and Mrs Ormond in memory of their brother, John S. Sargent 1929 (N04429)

Cat. 20

William Morris (1834–1896)

La Belle Iseult, 1857–8

Oil on canvas, 71.8 × 50.2 cm

Tate, London. Bequeathed by Miss May Morris 1939 (N04999)

Cat. 21

Edward Burne-Jones (1833–1898)

Fair Rosamund and Queen Eleanor, 1862

Ink, watercolour, gouache and gum on paper, 26 × 27.3 cm

Tate, London. Presented by J. R. Holliday through the Art Fund 1923 (N03822)

Cat. 22

Edward Burne-Jones (1833–1898)

One of seven studies for Queen Eleanor and Fair Rosamund, 1862

Pencil on paper, 24.6 × 22 cm

Victoria and Albert Museum, London. Bequeathed by J.R. Holliday (E.2857-1927)

Cat. 23

Edward Burne-Jones (1833–1898)

Study for St Valentine's Day, verso of Study for 'The Merciful Knight', about 1863

Graphite on paper, 25.8 × 17.8 cm

Tate, London. Bequeathed by J.R. Holliday 1927 (A00084)

Cat. 24

Dante Gabriel Rossetti (1828–1882)

Lucrezia Borgia, 1860–1

Graphite and watercolour on paper, 43.8 × 25.8 cm

Tate, London. Presented in memory of Henry Michael Field by Charles Ricketts through the Art Fund 1916 (N03063)

Cat. 25

Simeon Solomon (1840–1905)

A Youth relating Tales to Ladies, 1870

Oil on canvas, 35.5 × 53.4 cm

Tate, London. Presented by the Kretschmer family in accordance with the wishes of William Kretchmer 1983 (T03702)

Cat. 26

Convex mirror owned by Dante Gabriel Rossetti (1828–1882)

32.7 diameter × 4.8 cm

Society of Antiquaries of London, (Kelmscott Manor, KM 611)

Cat. 27

Henry Treffry Dunn (1838–1899)

Dante Gabriel Rossetti's Bedroom at Tudor House, 16 Cheyne Walk, 1872

Watercolour on paper, 33.5 cm diameter

Wightwick Manor, the National Trust. Given to the National Trust by Mrs Helen Annie Handford Guglielmini in 2001 (1287978)

Cat. 28

William Holman Hunt (1827–1910)

Il Dolce far Niente, 1859–66, reworked 1874–5

Oil on canvas, 99.1 × 80 cm

Private Collection

Cat. 29

Elizabeth Eleanor Siddall (1829–1862)

The Lady of Shalott, 1853

Pen, ink and pencil on paper, 24.8 × 17.8 cm

The Maas Gallery

Cat. 30

William Holman Hunt (1827–1910)

The Lady of Shalott, engraved by J.Thompson, published 1857

Wood engraving on paper, 9.5 × 7.9 cm

Tate, London. Presented by Harold Hartley 1925 (N04052)

Cat. 31

William Holman Hunt (1827–1910)

The Lady of Shalott, about 1886–1905

Oil on wood, 44.4 × 34.1 cm

Manchester Art Gallery (1934.401)

Cat. 32

John William Waterhouse (1849–1917)

The Lady of Shalott, 1894

Oil on canvas, 142.2 × 86.3 cm

Leeds Museums and Galleries (Leeds Art Gallery, LEEAG.1895.0004)

Cat. 33

Sidney Meteyard (1868–1947)

'I am Half-Sick of Shadows, Said the Lady of Shalott' 1913

Oil on canvas, 76 × 114.5 cm

Private Collection, courtesy of Martin Beisly

Cat. 34

Edward Burne-Jones (1833–1898)

Margaret Burne-Jones, 1885–6

Oil on canvas, 91.2 × 66 cm

Private Collection

Cat. 35

Charles Shannon (1863–1937)

The Bath of Venus, 1898–1904

Oil on canvas, 146 × 97.8 cm

Tate, London. Presented by Francis Howard 1940 (N05160)

Cat. 36

Charles Shannon (1863–1937)

Les Marmitons, 1897

Oil on canvas on board, 39 × 36.6 cm

Tate, London. Purchased 1942 (N05363)

Cat. 37

John Phillip (1817–1867)

Partial copy of 'Las Meninas', 1862

Oil on canvas, 185 × 148 cm

Royal Academy of Arts, London (03/1097)

Cat. 38

Wolfram Onslow Ford (1879–1956)

My Father, reproduction of the missing original printed in *The Studio,* vol. 25, 1902

Tate Archives, London (35885–1001)

Cat. 39

Convex mirror used by William Orpen (1878–1931)

63 diameter × 8 cm

Private Ownership

Cat. 40

William Orpen (1878–1931)

The Mirror, 1900

Oil on canvas, 50.8 × 40.6 cm

Tate, London. Presented by Mrs Coutts Michie through the Art Fund in memory of the George McCulloch Collection 1913 (N02940)

Cat. 41
William Orpen (1878–1931)
A Bloomsbury Family, 1907
Oil on canvas, 86.5 × 91.5 cm
Scottish National Gallery of Modern Art, Edinburgh (GMA 881)

Cat. 42
Arthur Studd (1863–1919)
Self Portrait in Round Mirror, early twentieth century
Pencil on paper, 13 × 11.5 cm
Private Collection

Cat. 43
Mark Gertler (1891–1939)
Still Life with Self Portrait, 1918
Oil on canvas, 50.8 × 40.6 cm
Leeds Museums and Galleries (Leeds Art Gallery, LEEAG. 1956.0001.0003)

LIST OF LENDERS

Edinburgh
Scottish National Gallery of Modern Art, Edinburgh

Leeds
Leeds Museums and Galleries (Leeds Art Gallery)

London
The Maas Gallery
Museum of London
Royal Academy of Arts
Society of Antiquaries of London (Kelmscott Manor)
Tate
Victoria and Albert Museum
Wilson Centre for Photography

Manchester
Manchester City Art Galleries

Wolverhampton
Wightwick Manor, the National Trust

We would also like to thank all lenders and private collectors who wish to remain anonymous

BIOGRAPHIES

John Phillip (1817–1867)
The Scottish artist John Phillip trained at the Royal Academy Schools in the late 1830s, when he and group of fellow students, united by friendship and disenchantment with the Royal Academy, formed themselves into a short-lived group known as 'The Clique'. After a spell in his native Aberdeen, where he specialised in portraiture and Highland scenes, he was advised to travel to the warmer climate of southern Europe for the sake of his delicate health, and he made three extended visits to Spain, in 1851, 1856 and 1860. There he encountered the work of Velázquez, which was to have a profound effect on his painting style. He also developed a speciality in colourful scenes of Spanish life, which proved popular and earned him the nickname 'Spanish' Phillip. Although Phillip was friendly with Millais, he was not particularly enthusiastic about the Pre-Raphaelite movement, and his mature work, like Millais's, is characterised by a broader, more painterly approach.

Ford Madox Brown (1821–1893)
Ford Madox Brown was born in Calais and studied in Bruges, Ghent and Antwerp before moving to Paris. A trip to Rome in 1845 brought him into contact with early Italian art and a group of German painters called the Nazarenes, who were aiming to revive Christian art based on late medieval prototypes. He returned to England in 1846, and developed a friendship with the slightly younger painters of the Pre-Raphaelite Brotherhood, even acting as Rossetti's tutor for a while. Brown was not invited to join the movement, but remained a close associate of the artists, adopting their brilliant palette and close-up realism in his own work. Like them, he tackled religious subjects and explored contemporary social themes. His *Last of England* (1855) was inspired by the emigration of the Pre-Raphaelite sculptor Thomas Woolner, and his mammoth canvas *Work* (1852–65) is a highly detailed celebration of the labour of different social classes. In 1861 Brown became a founder member of Morris, Marshall, Faulkner & Co. The major work of his later years was a cycle of paintings for Manchester Town Hall depicting the history of the city.

William Holman Hunt (1827–1910)
Hunt felt he was the only one of the group who remained faithful to the Pre-Raphaelites' stated aims throughout his career. He enrolled at the Royal Academy Schools in 1844 and co-founded the Pre-Raphaelite Brotherhood in 1848. His work was characterised by minute precision of handling, brilliance of colour and morally earnest subject matter. Many of his paintings were animated by a desire to promote Christian ideals, and in 1854 he embarked on a two-year journey to the Holy Land intending to paint biblical episodes in the locations where they had occurred. *The Scapegoat* (1854–5), showing an outcast animal on the shores of the Dead Sea, is the most famous work resulting from the trip. Following a broken engagement to artist's model Annie Miller, he married Fanny Waugh, who died in childbirth in 1866. Hunt married her sister, Edith, in 1875, and made a further trip to Jerusalem, where he maintained a studio. The artist became a venerated figure in the late Victorian and Edwardian art world, and one-man shows of his work were held in London, Manchester, Liverpool and Glasgow in 1906–7.

Dante Gabriel Rossetti (1828–1882)
Rossetti's father was an Italian poet and scholar, and Rossetti himself pursued parallel careers as a poet and an artist. He joined the Royal Academy Schools in 1845, and was also briefly taught by Ford Madox Brown. In 1848 he moved into a studio with William Holman Hunt and co-founded the Pre-Raphaelite Brotherhood. Rossetti's earliest works are religious subjects which adopt some of the features of fourteenth- and fifteenth-century Italian and Flemish painting. In the 1850s he produced some gem-like watercolours inspired by the poetry of Robert Browning, Dante, Arthurian romance and medieval legend. He met the slightly younger William Morris and Edward Burne-Jones in 1856, and they collaborated on murals for the Oxford

Union. Rossetti's muse and model in the 1850s was Elizabeth Siddall, whom he married in 1860. Following her death he had liaisons with other women who modelled for him, and he enjoyed a long-running intimate relationship with Morris's wife, Jane, who posed for some of his best-known paintings. In the last two decades of his life Rossetti painted large-scale sensual oil paintings of beautiful women, often with literary or mythological references. He became increasingly reclusive in his later years, withdrawing to his house in Cheyne Walk, Chelsea, his eccentricity exacerbated by depression and addiction.

John Everett Millais (1829–1896)

A child prodigy, Millais became the youngest-ever student at the Royal Academy Schools when he enrolled in 1840. Following his meeting with fellow students Rossetti and Hunt, he became the third founder-member of the Pre-Raphaelite Brotherhood in 1848. While an early work, *Christ in the House of his Parents*, was roundly criticised (notably by Charles Dickens) when it was exhibited in 1850, Millais enjoyed considerable success for most his career. In 1854 he married John Ruskin's former wife, Effie Gray, with whom he had fallen in love while holidaying in Scotland. At about that time his painting style began to change from the meticulously detailed Pre-Raphaelite way of working to a broader manner, which enabled him to be far more productive. He also became a prolific illustrator for numerous publications, including the Moxon edition of Tennyson's poems. Millais's paintings of uplifting narrative scenes, beautiful young women and children earned him great popularity and a large income, and he developed a flourishing practice as a portraitist in the 1870s. He was the first artist to be awarded a baronetcy in 1885, and shortly before his death he was elected President of the Royal Academy.

Elizabeth Eleanor Siddall (1829–1862)

Elizabeth Eleanor Siddall first entered Pre-Raphaelite circles as an artists' model: her striking features and mass of copper-coloured hair are familiar from a number of Pre-Raphaelite works, including Millais's *Ophelia* (1852). After she became Rossetti's muse and lover she modelled exclusively for him, and he drew and painted her obsessively. Siddall was also an artist and poet in her own right, although she had no formal training. She began producing drawings and watercolours in 1852 and made over 100 works in the following 10 years. Her style was close to Rossetti's (the two sometimes collaborated) and characterised by flattened forms and bright colours. Her literary, medieval, and chivalric subjects, often with female protagonists, were admired by John Ruskin, who paid her a monthly retainer. Elizabeth Siddall died of an overdose of laudanum in 1862, shortly after giving birth to a stillborn daughter. After her death Rossetti painted a tribute to her, *Beata Beatrix* (about 1864–70), in which she is shown as Dante's muse, Beatrice.

Edward Burne-Jones (1833–1898)

Burne-Jones was a leading artist in the second phase of the Pre-Raphaelite movement, celebrated for his dreamily romantic scenes drawn from classical legend, fantasy and chivalric lore. At Oxford he and his fellow student William Morris came under the influence of Ruskin and the first generation of Pre-Raphaelites, deciding to devote themselves to art. Burne-Jones formed a particularly close association with Rossetti, who had a notable impact on his early drawings and watercolours. Right from the start, Burne-Jones was a prolific designer of stained glass and other forms of decorative art, and he became a founder member of Morris, Marshall, Faulkner & Co in 1861. Visits to Italy in 1859, 1862, 1871 and 1873 brought him into direct contact with Italian art, and his close study of Italian Renaissance works from the time of Raphael is evident in his work from the 1860s onwards. An exhibition of eight paintings at the Grosvenor Gallery in 1877 established him as a key figure in the Aesthetic movement, and from the 1890s his work attracted an audience in Europe and America, becoming particularly admired in Symbolist circles. In 1894 he was awarded a baronetcy.

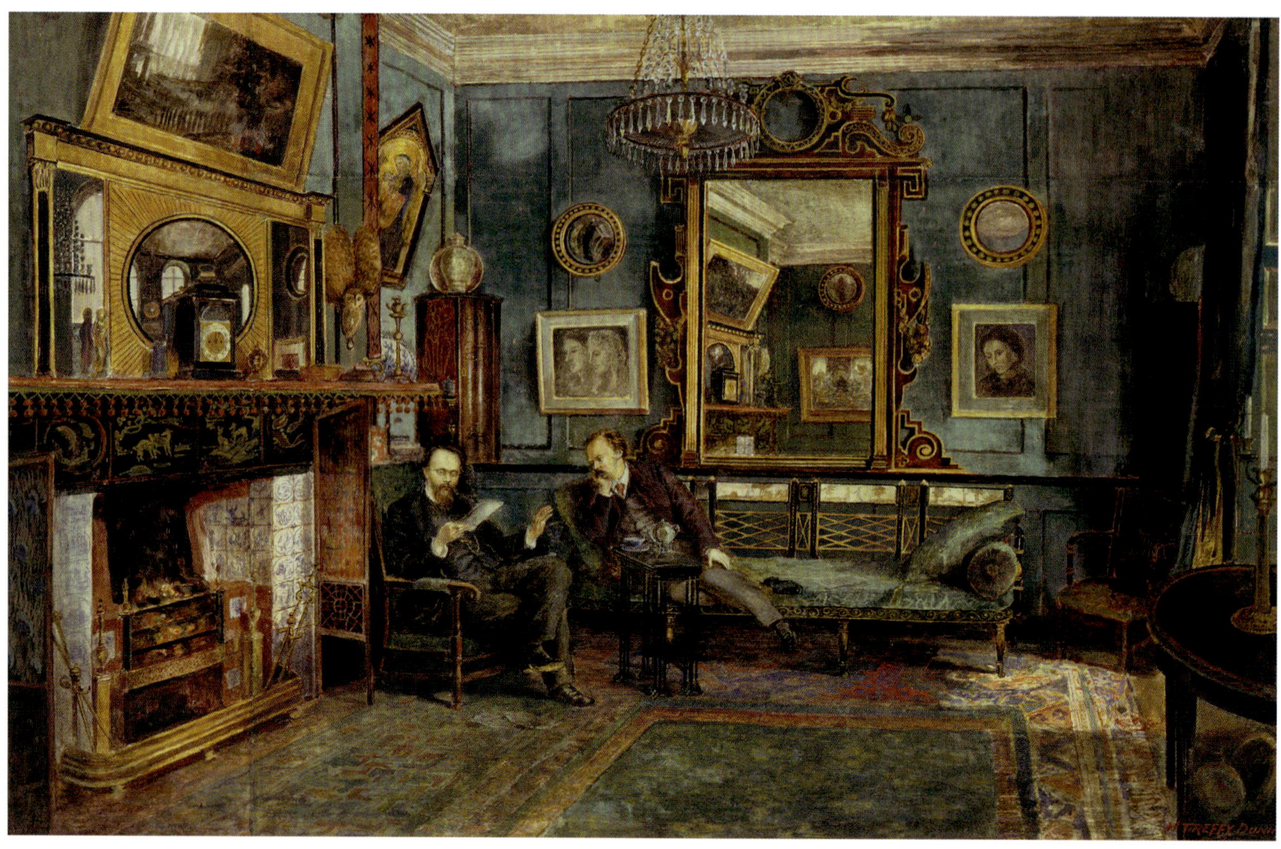

Fig. 19
Henry Treffry Dunn (1838–1899)
Dante Gabriel Rossetti and Theodore Watts-Dunton at home in 16 Cheyne Walk, 1882
Gouache and watercolour on paper, now on card, 54.3 x 81.9 cm
National Portrait Gallery, London (NPG 3022) (The portrait of Rossetti is posthumous)

William Morris (1834–1896)

Multi-talented, William Morris was a designer, craftsman, writer, poet and social reformer. As a student at Oxford, where he met his lifelong friend Burne-Jones, he developed a fascination with medieval art, literature and architecture, as well as the writings of John Ruskin, which led to his introduction to the artists of the Pre-Raphaelite Brotherhood. In 1859 Morris married Jane Burden, and the couple moved to the Red House in Bexley Heath, which had been designed for them by Morris's friend Philip Webb in an eclectic neo-Gothic style. In 1865 they moved back to London, taking the lease with Rossetti on the medieval Kelmscott Manor in Oxfordshire as their country home in 1871. By the time he founded his design company, Morris, Marshall, Faulkner and Co. in 1861, Morris had abandoned painting to concentrate instead on the design and production of furniture, tapestry, stained glass, fabrics, wallpaper, carpets and ceramics. The company was run along the lines of a medieval guild, with the intention that craftsmen should both design and execute their work. Morris's ideas and practice bore lasting fruit in the English Arts and Crafts movement. In 1884 he co-founded the Socialist League, devoting much of his time to political activism as well as poetry, translation and his private Kelmscott Press.

Henry Treffry Dunn (1838–1899)

Trained at Heatherly's School of Fine Art in Chelsea, Treffry Dunn became Rossetti's studio and personal assistant in 1867 and stayed with him until around 1878, when he left following an argument over his unpaid salary. While he was a skilful artist he remained in Rossetti's shadow, his own work showing the unmistakable imprint of his master. For the most part he made preliminary studies for Rossetti and copies of his paintings, to which Rossetti would add the final touches. After Rossetti's death, Treffry Dunn was employed to look after the house in Cheyne Walk and to prepare for the studio sale. He had previously produced watercolours of four of the rooms, which are an invaluable source of information on the house's distinctive interior and supplement his written *Recollections of Dante Gabriel Rossetti and His Circle*, which describe aspects of life in the Rossetti household.

Simeon Solomon (1840–1905)
The youngest of eight children in an orthodox Jewish family, Simeon Solomon was only a child when the Pre-Raphaelite Brotherhood was founded. He entered the Royal Academy Schools in 1855 and was drawn into the circle around Rossetti and Burne-Jones, adopting many features of their style in his own paintings and drawings. In the 1860s he developed a reputation as a book illustrator and undertook decorative work for William Morris and William Burges. Solomon's earliest works illustrate literary subjects, Hebraic history and ritual, but he later turned to classical themes, often overlaying them with a strongly homoerotic flavour. In 1873 he was arrested for sodomy and essentially disowned by the Pre-Raphaelite circle, although a circle of devotees that included the poet Algernon Swinburne and Oscar Wilde continued to admire his work. He spent the last few years of his life in a workhouse, his health blighted by alcoholism.

John William Waterhouse
(1849–1917)
Although Waterhouse was born the year after the foundation of the Pre-Raphaelite Brotherhood, he embraced the type of literary subjects they favoured long after the movement's heyday. However, he never adopted the artists' hard-edged minutely detailed technique, preferring a broader manner of painting that he had learnt from the French painter Jules Bastien-Lepage. Waterhouse spent his early childhood in Italy, returning to England in 1854 and later entering the Royal Academy Schools. His first works were Italian subjects and scenes from Ancient Greece and classical mythology that bear some similarity to the paintings of Laurence Alma-Tadema, and he had an enduring fascination with the theme of the female enchantress. He depicted a favourite Pre-Raphaelite subject, The Lady of Shalott, on three occasions, and late in his career produced a series of paintings of Ophelia, perhaps inspired by Millais's and Rossetti's treatments of the theme.

Charles Shannon (1863–1937)
Shannon studied at the City and Guilds Art School in Kennington, London, and it was here that he met his lifelong artistic and personal partner, Charles Ricketts (1866–1931). The pair worked together, designing and illustrating books, founding the magazine *The Dial* in 1889, and launching the Vale Press in 1894. They were key figures in the London art world of the 1890s, mixing with such prominent figures as Oscar Wilde and the illustrator Edmund Dulac. Shannon's paintings – mainly imaginative subjects and portraits – were often based on his lithographic work, and heavily influenced by Venetian art. He was elected Associate of the Royal Academy in 1911, and exhibited at the Academy from 1912 until 1930. He and Ricketts were also significant collectors of Old Master drawings and paintings, Egyptian and Greek antiquities, Japanese woodblock prints and Persian miniatures. Their collection now belongs to the Fitzwilliam Museum, Cambridge.

Arthur Studd (1863–1919)
Arthur Studd studied at the Slade School of Art under the French artist Alphonse Legros and at the Académie Julian in Paris, where he met James McNeill Whistler. Back in London, he moved to Cheyne Walk in Chelsea and the two artists became neighbours. Studd referred to Whistler as 'the Master', and adopted his muted palette, restricted colour range and some of his subject matter. However, he failed to persuade Whistler to join him in Tahiti when he went to paint there in the company of Gauguin in 1897–8. Studd's private income allowed him to collect art, and he bought a number of Whistler's paintings, three of which are now in the Tate collection.

Sidney Meteyard (1868–1947)
Meteyard was one of the Birmingham Group of artists who worked in a revived Pre-Raphaelite manner that was strongly influenced by Burne-Jones and the Arts and Crafts movement. He studied at Birmingham School of Art, and was among the students chosen to paint murals for Birmingham Town Hall in 1890. Meteyard taught at the School of Art for 45 years, specialising in life drawing, as well as crafts that included enamelling, gesso and leatherwork. He also designed stained glass and produced book illustrations, often in collaboration with his wife, Kate Eadie.

William Orpen (1878–1931)
Orpen was an Irish artist who trained at the Slade School in London and went on to become one of the most successful and prolific portrait painters in Edwardian Britain. Like his friend Augustus John, he adopted a painterly style and bravura brushwork which reflected his admiration for the Old Masters, especially Velázquez. Orpen's portrait practice brought him riches, although there was a decline in his critical fortunes after his death. Nonetheless, some of his self portraits, in which he scrutinised his own appearance and sometimes poked fun at himself in the guise of different characters, have an engaging depth. In 1917 Orpen was appointed Official War Artist, producing memorable visual records of life in the trenches. In 1919 he was appointed an official artist to the British Peace Delegation, and he painted the large and very traditional group portrait, *The Signing of Peace in the Hall of Mirrors, Versailles, 28th June 1919*.

Wolfram Onslow Ford (1879–1956)
The son of the sculptor and President of the Art Workers Guild, Edward Onslow Ford, Wolfram Onslow Ford was an artist of modest success who studied at the Royal Academy and was known chiefly as a portraitist. His sitters included his father, Whistler and an Indian price. He also painted several rural scenes.

Mark Gertler (1891–1939)
Mark Gertler was born into a family of Polish Jewish immigrants in the East End of London and spent his early childhood in extreme poverty. He trained at the Slade School of Art, where he won several scholarships and prizes and fell in unrequited love with fellow student, Dora Carrington, who introduced him to the upper-class Bloomsbury Group. Gertler's style was highly individual and drew upon elements of Eastern European folk art. Many of his paintings portray the enclosed world and hardship of a Jewish ghetto. His masterpiece *Merry-go-round* (1916), which shows wounded soldiers and their companions on fairground horses spinning around endlessly in a grotesque parody of gaiety, was painted at the height of war and it is hard not to see its brutal mood and harsh colours as a reflection of his anti-militarist sentiments. Gertler was persistently dogged by ill-health and depression, and took his own life in 1939.

NOTES

JAN VAN EYCK'S ARNOLFINI PORTRAIT

Susan Foister

1. See Billinge, Campbell, Dunkerton, Foister, Kirby, Pilc, Roy, Spring and White 1997, p. 40.
2. For full catalogue entries on all three works by Jan van Eyck in the National Gallery see Campbell 1998
3. See Campbell 1998, pp. 198–9.
4. Panofsky 1934, pp. 117–19; 122–7. Panofsky 1953, pp. 201–3.
5. Campbell 1998, pp. 201, 191.
6. See Campbell 1998, pp. 174–8 for detailed references to provenance.

THE ARNOLFINI PORTRAIT IN THE NINETEENTH CENTURY:

RECEPTION AND REPRODUCTION

Anna Koopstra

1. For an insightful analysis of the issues touched upon here see Graham 2007. For a detailed account of the history of the painting see also Hicks 2012.
2. NG archive, NGA02/4/2/228. Also cited by Campbell 1998, p. 176.
3. Cited by Campbell 1998, pp. 176–8.
4. NG archive, NG5/50/1. I thank Susanna Avery-Quash for alerting me to this letter and Richard Wragg for retrieving it for me.
5. On 11 September 1846, *The Times* reported that in the year the portrait went on display (1843) the Gallery had received 456,195 visitors; this rose to 696,245 in 1845.
6. Felix Summerly was the pseudonym of Sir Henry Cole (1808–1882), who would become the first director of the South Kensington Museum (later renamed the Victoria and Albert Museum) in 1855.
7. Shortly after the first public auction of Aders's collection took place in 1835, the National Gallery was offered the copy, but it refused to purchase the work. For the early and modern history of the *Ghent Altarpiece* see S. Kemperdick and J. Rössler in Berlin 2015.
8. The sketchbook in the V&A contains several drawings which have been identified as copies after illustrations from publications from the eighteenth and nineteenth century, copies of manuscript illuminations and sketches from works by Lucas Cranach, Marcantonio Raimondi, the della Robbias and Antonio Rossellino. See also Graham 2007, p. 114.
9. The nude figures of Adam and Eve were published separately, an indication of the taste and morals of the time.
10. *Athenaeum*, 25 March 1843, p. 291.
11. *Athenaeum*, 3 July 1841, p. 509.
12. *Illustrated London News*, 15 April 1843, p. 257.
13. In 1847 the first descriptive and historical catalogue of the pictures in the National Gallery with biographic notices of the painters by Ralph N. Wornum and revised by Charles L. Eastlake appeared; the identification of the Arnolfinis was first included in this descriptive catalogue in 1862. Campbell 1998, the latest catalogue on the Gallery's fifteenth-century Netherlandish paintings, publishes extensive research on which male member of the Arnolfini family is actually depicted.
14. Campbell 1998, p. 204.

THE PRE-RAPHAELITES AND THE ARNOLFINI PORTRAIT

A NEW VISUAL WORLD

Alison Smith

1. J.A. Crowe and G.B. Cavalcaselle's *The Early Flemish Painters*, which provided the first English monograph on van Eyck, was published in 1857.
2. *The Crayon*, August 1856, pp. 236–9. In the story Stephens offers

an explanation of the two additional figures in the mirror. Art historian Robert Wilkes has suggested the date of 1850 based on William Michael Rossetti's mention of 'a tale of a medieval musician' in *The PRB Journal,* 2 December 1850 (correspondence with the author, 25 November 2016).

3. Fredeman 1975, p. 107.
4. Hunt 1905, vol. 1, p. 54; Burne-Jones 1904, vol. 2, p. 306.
5. Cited in Rossetti 1895, vol.1, p. 135.
6. Eastlake 1847, p. 223. See also Ruskin *Works*, XII, pp. 256.
7. Ruskin *Works*, XII, p. 408.
8. For an analysis of Pre-Raphaelite painting techniques and materials see Townsend, Ridge and Hackney 2004.
9. Quoted in Bryden 1998, vol. 2, p. 162; Rossetti 1895, vol. 1, pp. 142–3.
10. *The Art Journal*, 1859, p. 132. For an in-depth analysis of the influence of early Northern painting on the Pre-Raphaelites see Langley 1995, pp. 501–8; Warner 1992, pp. 1–11.
11. Ruskin *Works*, XXXVI, letter to D.G. Rossetti 1865, p. 409; Thomas Sulman, 'A Memorable Art Class', *Good Words*, August 1897, p. 550, cited in Graham 2007, p. 142.
12. 'Pre-Raphaelitism': Lecture delivered 18 November 1853, Ruskin *Works*, XII, p. 157.
13. 'Les Beaux-Arts en Europe', translated in *Fraser's Magazine*, June 1856, p. 691.
14. G.T. Robinson, 'Suggestions in Decorative Design from the Works of Great Painters', *The Art Journal*, December 1884, p. 358; Kinchin 2008–9, p. 68.
15. Haweis 1881, p. 250.
16. 'The Awakening Conscience', letter to the editor of *The Times*, 25 May 1854, Ruskin *Works* XII, p. 334.
17. Charles Aitkin, 'English 19th Century Art at the National Gallery', *The Burlington Magazine*, July 1917, p. 3.
18. Burne-Jones 1904, vol. 1, p. 215.
19. H.C. Marillier, *Dante Gabriel Rossetti: An Illustrated Memorial of his Art and Life 1901*, p. 79.
20. *The valuable contents of the residence of Dante Gabriel Rossetti...sold by auction on... July 5, 6, 7* 1882.
21. Robertson 1931, p. 73.
22. Townsend and Poulson 2008, pp. 167–8.
23. Hunt 1913, vol. 2, p. 401.
24. Prettejohn 2000, p. 262.
25. Rossetti was the focus of two exhibitions in 1883 at the Burlington Fine Arts Club and Royal Academy; the first Millais retrospective was at the Grosvenor Gallery in 1886 followed by the large exhibition organised by the Royal Academy after his death in 1898. A survey of Hunt's work was presented by the Fine Art Society in 1886.
26. London 1989, p. 109; Lago 1981, p. 136.
27. *Pall Mall Gazette*, 5 May 1887, p. 82.
28. Graham 2007, p. 126; p. 177.
29. Rothenstein 1952, p. 218.

Fig. 20, detail of fig. 9, p. 40

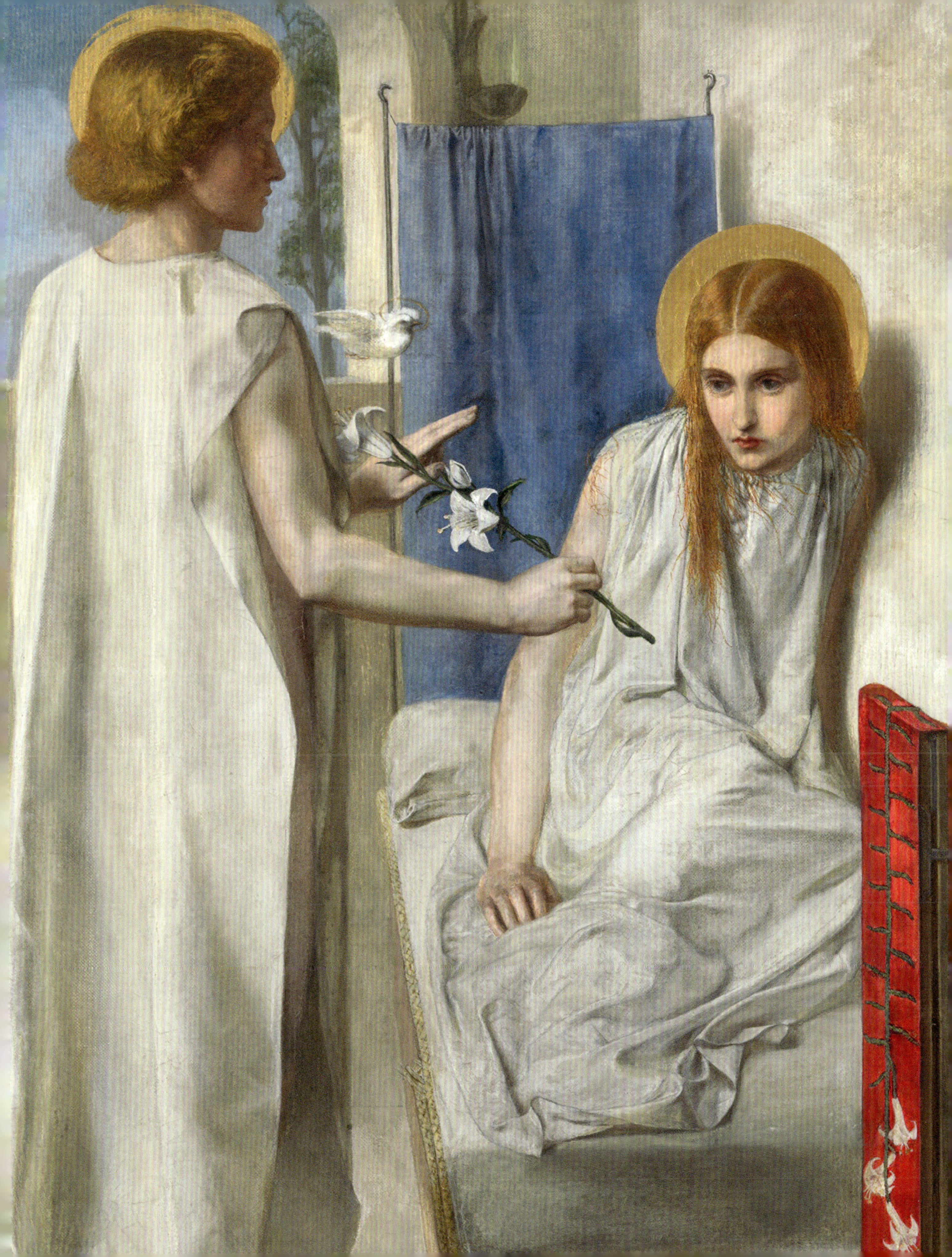

BIBLIOGRAPHY

Armstrong 2008
I. Armstrong, *Victorian Glass Worlds: Glass Culture and the Imagination 1830–1880,* Oxford 2008

Billinge, Campbell, Dunkerton, Foister, Kirby, Pilc, Roy, Spring and White 1997
R. Billinge, L. Campbell, J. Dunkerton, S. Foister, J. Kirby, J. Pilc, A. Roy, M. Spring and R. White, 'Methods and Materials of Northern European Painting in the National Gallery, 1400–1550', *National Gallery Technical Bulletin*, vol. 18, 1997, pp. 6–55

Berlin 2015
S. Kemperdick and J. Rössler, *The Ghent Altarpiece by the Brothers Van Eyck. History and Appraisal*, exh. cat., Berlin (Gemäldegalerie) 2015

Bronkhurst 2006
J. Bronkhurst, *William Holman Hunt: A Catalogue Raisonné*, London 2006

Bryden 1998
I. Bryden, *The Pre-Raphaelites: Writings and Sources*, 4 vols, London 1998

Burne-Jones 1904
G. Burne-Jones, *Memorials of Edward Burne-Jones*, 2 vols, London 1904

Campbell 1998
L. Campbell, *The Fifteenth-Century Netherlandish Schools* (National Gallery catalogues), London 1998

Eastlake 1847
C.L. Eastlake, *Materials for a History of Oil Painting*, London 1847

Fredeman 1975
W.E. Fredeman, *The PRB Journal: William Michael Rossetti's Diary of the PRB 1849–1953*, Oxford 1975

Graham 2007
J. Graham, *Inventing van Eyck: The Remaking of an Artist for the Modern Age*, Oxford and New York 2007

Haweis 1881
H.R. Haweis, *The Art of Decoration*, London 1881

Hicks 2012
C. Hicks, *Girl in a Green Dress: The History and Mystery of the Arnolfini Portrait*, London 2012

Hunt 1905–1913
W.H. Hunt, *Pre-Raphaelitism and the Pre-Raphaelite Brotherhood*, 2 vols, London 1905 and 1913

Kinchin 2008
J. Kinchin, 'Performance and the Reflected Self: Modern Stagings of Domestic Space, 1860–1914', *Studies in the Decorative Arts*, vol. 16, no. 1 (Fall–Winter 2008–9), pp. 64–91

Lago 1981
M. Lago (ed.), *Burne-Jones Talking*, London 1981

Langley 1995
J. Langley, 'Pre-Raphaelites or ante-Dürerites?' *The Burlington Magazine*, August 1995, pp. 501–8

London 1989
J. Christian, *The Last Romantics: The Romantic Tradition in British Art, Burne-Jones to Stanley Spencer*, exh. cat., London (Barbican Art Gallery) 1989

London 1998
J. Miller, *On Reflection*, exh. cat., London (National Gallery) 1998

London 2007
J. Rosenfeld and A. Smith, *Millais*, exh. cat., London (Tate Britain) 2007

London 2012
T. Barringer, J. Rosenfeld and A. Smith, *Pre-Raphaelites: Victorian Avant-Garde*, exh. cat., London (Tate Britain) 2012

Monteiro 2008
S. Monteiro, 'Veiling the Mechanical Eye: Antoine Claudet and the Spectacle of Photography in Victorian London', *Interdisciplinary Studies in the Long Nineteenth Century*, vol. 7, 2008 www.19.bbk.ac.uk

Panofsky 1934
E. Panofsky, 'Jan van Eyck's Arnolfini Portrait', *The Burlington Magazine*, March 1934, pp. 117–19; 122–7

Panofsky 1953
E. Panofsky, *Early Netherlandish Painting, its Origins and Character,* Cambridge (MA) 1953

Prettejohn 2000
E. Prettejohn, *The Art of the Pre-Raphaelites*, London 2000

Prettejohn 2017
E. Prettejohn, *Modern Painters, Old Masters: The Art of Imitation from the Pre-Raphaelites to the First World War*, New Haven and London 2017

Robertson 1931
W.G. Robertson, *Time Was*, London 1931

Rossetti 1895
W.M. Rossetti (ed.), *Dante Gabriel Rossetti: His Family Letters, with a Memoir*, 2 vols, London 1895

Rothenstein 1952
J. Rothenstein, *Modern English Painters: Sickert to Smith*, London 1952

Ruskin Works
J. Ruskin, *Library Edition of the Collected Works of John Ruskin*, eds E.T. Cook and A. Wedderburn, 39 vols, London 1903–12

Townsend, Ridge and Hackney 2004
J.H. Townsend, J. Ridge and S. Hackney, *Pre-Raphaelite Painting Techniques*, London 2004

Townsend and Poulson 2008
J.H. Townsend and J. Poulson, 'Painting: Materials and Method' in *Holman Hunt and the Pre-Raphaelite Vision*, eds K. Lochnan and C. Jacobi, New Haven 2008

Warner 1992
M. Warner, 'The Pre-Raphaelites and the National Gallery', in *The Pre-Raphaelites in Context*, San Marino (CA) 1992, pp. 1–11

Yearwood 2014
C.E. Yearwood, *The Looking-Glass World: Mirrors in Pre-Raphaelite Painting 1850–1915*, PhD thesis, University of York 2014

ACKNOWLEDGEMENTS

The authors wish to thank the following colleagues for their kind assistance and expertise

Susanna Avery-Quash
Penelope Curtis
Julia Dudkiewicz
Jonathan Franklin
Carol Jacobi
Hope Kingsley
Rupert Maas
Rebecca Milner
Zara Moran
Elizabeth Prettejohn
Marika Spring
Joyce Townsend
Nicholas Tromans
Richard Wragg
Claire Yearwood

INDEX

Page numbers in *italics* refer to illustrations

CREDITS

This edition published in Great Britain in 2017 by
National Gallery Company Limited
St Vincent House
30 Orange Street
London WC2H 7HH
www.nationalgallery.co.uk

9781857096194
1044203

British Library Cataloguing-in-Publication Data. A catalogue record is available from the British Library.

Library of Congress Control Number: 2017939573

Publisher: Jan Green
Project Editor: Claire Young
Editor: Caroline Bugler
Picture Researcher: Suzanne Bosman
Production: Jane Hyne and Amanda Mackie
Designed by LAWN, Liverpool
Colour reproductions by Altaimage, London
Printed in Italy by Conti Tipocolor

All measurements give height before width

Photographic credits

Bruges
Groeningemuseum, Stedelijke Musea Brugge © Lukas – Art in Flanders VZW / Bridgeman Images: fig. 2.

Edinburgh
Scottish National Gallery of Modern Art, Edinburgh © National Galleries of Scotland: cat. 41.

Ghent
St Bavo © Lukas - Art in Flanders VZW / Bridgeman Images: fig. 3.

Kelmscott Manor © Kelmscott Manor / Bridgeman Images: fig. 12; © Society of Antiquaries of London (Kelmscott Manor). Photograph: Andy Stammers Photography: cat. 26.

Leeds
Leeds Museums and Galleries (Temple Newsam) © Leeds Museums and Galleries (Leeds Art Gallery) / Bridgeman Images: cats 32, 43; figs 1, 16, 18.

London
The Maas Gallery © Photo courtesy of the owner: cats 9, 29. © The National Gallery, London: cats 1, 2, 3, 4, 6, 7, 8; fig. 8. © The National Portrait Gallery, London: fig. 19. © Royal Academy of Arts, London: cat. 37. © Tate, London 2016: cats 13, 14, 16, 18, 19, 20, 21, 23, 24, 25, 30, 35, 36, 40; figs 4, 5, 6, 7, 9, 13, 20. Victoria and Albert Museum, London © V&A Images / Victoria and Albert Museum, London: cats 10, 17, 22. Wilson Centre for Photography, London © Photo courtesy of the owner: cats 11, 12, 15.

Madrid
Museo Nacional del Prado, Madrid © Photo MNP / Scala, Florence: fig. 15.

Manchester
Manchester Art Gallery © Manchester City Galleries / Bridgeman Images: cat. 31.

Melbourne
National Gallery of Victoria, Melbourne © National Gallery of Victoria, Melbourne / Bridgeman Images: fig. 14.

Vienna
Kunsthistorisches Museum, Vienna © Kunsthistorisches Museum, Vienna / Bridgeman Images: fig. 11.

Wightwick Manor / The National Trust © National Trust Images / John Hammond: cat. 27.

Private collections © Photo courtesy of the owners: cats 5, 28, 33, 34, 38, 39, 42; figs 10, 17.